Devil's Advocates

DEVIL'S ADVOCATES is a series of books devoted to exploring the classics of horror cinema. Contributors to the series come from the fields of teaching, academia, journalism and fiction, but all have one thing in common: a passion for the horror film and a desire to share it with the widest possible audience.

'The admirable Devil's Advocates series is not only essential – and fun – reading for the serious horror fan but should be set texts on any genre course.'
Dr Ian Hunter, Reader in Film Studies, De Montfort University, Leicester

'Auteur Publishing's new Devil's Advocates critiques on individual titles... offer bracingly fresh perspectives from passionate writers. The series will perfectly complement the BFI archive volumes.' **Christopher Fowler,** *Independent on Sunday*

'Devil's Advocates has proven itself more than capable of producing impassioned, intelligent analyses of genre cinema... quickly becoming the go-to guys for intelligent, easily digestible film criticism.' ***Horror Talk.com***

'Auteur Publishing continue the good work of giving serious critical attention to significant horror films.' *Black Static*

 DevilsAdvocatesbooks

DevilsAdBooks

ALSO AVAILABLE IN THIS SERIES

A Girl Walks Home Alone at Night Farshid Kazemi

Black Sunday Martyn Conterio

The Blair Witch Project Peter Turner

Blood and Black Lace Roberto Curti

The Blood on Satan's Claw David Evans-Powell

The Cabin in the Woods Susanne Kord

Candyman Jon Towlson

Cannibal Holocaust Calum Waddell

Cape Fear Rob Daniel

Carrie Neil Mitchell

The Company of Wolves James Gracey

The Conjuring Kevin J. Wetmore Jr.

Creepshow Simon Brown

Cruising Eugenio Ercolani & Marcus Stiglegger

The Curse of Frankenstein Marcus K. Harmes

Daughters of Darkness Kat Ellinger

Dawn of the Dead Jon Towlson

Dead of Night Jez Conolly & David Bates

The Descent James Marriot

The Devils Darren Arnold

Don't Look Now Jessica Gildersleeve

The Evil Dead Lloyd Haynes

The Fly Emma Westwood

Frenzy Ian Cooper

Halloween Murray Leeder

House of Usher Evert Jan van Leeuwen

In the Mouth of Madness Michael Blyth

IT: Chapters 1 & 2 Alissa Burger

It Follows Joshua Grimm

Ju-on The Grudge Marisa Hayes

Let the Right One In Anne Billson

M Samm Deighan

Macbeth Rebekah Owens

The Mummy Doris V. Sutherland

Nosferatu Cristina Massaccesi

The Omen Adrian Schober

Peeping Tom Kiri Bloom Walden

Pet Sematary Shellie McMurdo

Possession Alison Taylor

Prevenge Andrew Graves

Re-Animator Eddie Falvey

Repulsion Jeremy Carr

Saw Benjamin Poole

Scream Steven West

The Shining Laura Mee

Shivers Luke Aspell

The Silence of the Lambs Barry Forshaw

Snuff Mark McKenna

Suspiria Alexandra Heller-Nicholas

The Texas Chain Saw Massacre James Rose

The Thing Jez Conolly

Trouble Every Day Kate Robertson

Twin Peaks: Fire Walk With Me Lindsay Hallam

The Witch Brandon Grafius

Witchfinder General Ian Cooper

FORTHCOMING

Poltergeist Rob McLaughlin

I Walked with a Zombie Clive Dawson

The Wicker Man Steve A. Wiggins

Devil's Advocates

The Craft

Miranda Corcoran

First published in 2023 by
Auteur, an imprint of
Liverpool University Press,
4 Cambridge Street,
Liverpool
L69 7ZU

Series design: Nikki Hamlett at Cassels Design
Set by Cassels Design, Luton UK
Printed and bound by CPI Group (UK) Ltd, Croydon CR0 4YY

All rights reserved. No part of this publication may be reproduced in any material form (including photocopying or storing in any medium by electronic means and whether or not transiently or incidentally to some other use of this publication) without the permission of the copyright owner.

British Library Cataloguing-in-Publication Data
A catalogue record for this book is available from the British Library

ISBN hardback: 978-1-802-07724-7
eISBN: 978-1-802-07905-0

CONTENTS

Figures vi

Introduction 1

Chapter 1: From Reaganism to Riots: Situating *The Craft* in the 1990s 17

Chapter 2: "Satanic Panic": A New Witch for the Nineties 41

Chapter 3: "We are the weirdos, mister": Witchcraft and Identity Politics 69

Conclusion 99

Bibliography 107

FIGURES

Figure 1. Promotional poster 3

Figure 2. Rochelle, Nancy and Bonnie chanting in the gazebo 9

Figure 3. The famous "light as a feather, stiff as a board" sequence 11

Figure 4. The witches visit downtown Los Angeles 21

Figure 5. *The Virgin of Guadalupe (Virgen de Guadalupe)*
by Manuel de Arellano (1691) 23

Figure 6. *Witch Riding on a Goat* by Albrecht Dürer (1500) 43

Figure 7. The girls watch the popular 1960s sitcom *Bewitched* 47

Figure 8. Good vs bad witches in *The Wizard of Oz* (1939) 51

Figure 9. Domestic witch Jennifer (Veronica Lake) in *I Married a Witch* (1942) 53

Figure 10. Modern witch Gillian (Kim Novak) with the object of her affection Shep
(Jimmy Stewart) and her "familiar" Pyewacket 54

Figure 11. The witches travel to their initiation 69

Figure 12. Nancy is punished for her pursuit of power 74

Introduction

When I was 12 years old, I tried to form a coven with some of the other girls in my neighbourhood. After traipsing through a dense thicket, we found a clearing, surrounded by trees and shielded by heavy foliage. Although we were close enough to our respective homes to hear the buzz of neighbourhood gossip and the cries of children playing in the street, we felt as if we had found some secluded sylvan glade. We imagined that here, amidst the leaves and fallen pinecones, we were shielded by the protective boughs of nature. I don't remember what kind of magic we attempted, perhaps we just chanted or cast a circle. However, I do remember that after our brush with the mystical, we sat on the ground and shared a large box of chocolates. This memory remains with me, 20 years later, not because of our brief dalliance with the occult, but rather because of how that exploration of the preternatural was connected to the simple, girlish act of chatting and eating chocolate. I had recently seen *The Craft*, a film about witches who were not wizened hags or inhabitants of distant fantasy lands. Instead, they were simply teenage girls who, in addition to casting spells and invoking potent spirits, went shopping, had sleepovers and giggled about boys. As a preteen, *The Craft*'s use of witchcraft as a metaphor for teenage girlhood intrigued me as I simultaneously dreaded and craved the volatility of teen relationships, the independence of high school and the complex rituals associated with make-up and fashion. Like many other girls and young women, I was drawn to *The Craft* not simply because of its representation of witchcraft, but because of how its concern with the occult was interwoven with a nuanced, sympathetic portrayal of female adolescence.

In recent years, as the film accrued an ever more devout cult following, it has become apparent that for many viewers, especially young women, *The Craft*'s appeal lies in its unique status as a horror film that takes seriously the concerns of young women. While *The Craft* has exerted an immense influence over subsequent popular culture – traces of the film can be seen in *Buffy the Vampire Slayer* (1997–2003), *Charmed* (1998–2006) and *The Chilling Adventures of Sabrina* (2018–2020) – its true legacy can be found in how it affected generations of teenage girls, many of whom have held *The Craft* close to their hearts well into adulthood. In addition to forming an emotional bond with the film, many young viewers of *The Craft* were inspired to explore witchcraft, Wicca and Neopagan faiths in search of an authentic, alternative spirituality. Scholar Peg Aloi has described *The*

Craft as "the single greatest influence on the growth of teenage Witchcraft in America" (118). *The Craft*, then, is a film that has exerted both a pop-cultural and a real-world influence, shaping the way in which many individuals have thought about questions of girlhood, power and friendship, as well as igniting mainstream interest in witchcraft.

The Craft was not the first horror film to employ the preternatural as a means of exploring the adolescent experience. *The Exorcist* (1973) and *Carrie* (1976) rendered the teen girl monstrous two decades before the release of *The Craft*, while as early as the 1950s, *I Was a Teenage Werewolf* (1957) reimagined the awkward physicality of adolescence in terms of lycanthropic transformation. Nevertheless, there is something unique about *The Craft*. It is not only a film about teenage girls, but a film *for* teenage girls. It engages self-consciously with contemporary teen culture, incorporating popular music and fashion into its grungy, goth aesthetic. Its main characters are also distinct individuals. Coming from diverse backgrounds, they each embody unique aspects of the adolescent experience. Moreover, while *The Craft*'s witches are flawed figures, they ultimately refuse the passivity often ascribed to women on screen. They are not possessed or afflicted with powers they don't want; rather, they seek out power and claim it for themselves. The four teen witches support one another and create a sisterhood apart from the abuses, trials and humiliations of adolescence – a space where they can be themselves. At the same time, they can be cruel to each other, betraying trust and behaving selfishly. It is this duality, the capacity for infinite love and infinite cruelty, that perhaps most accurately reflects the intensity of female adolescence and the ardency of its friendships.

Like its main characters, *The Craft* is itself a flawed, complex film. Its progressive portrayals of female empowerment are often hampered by stereotypical representations of girlish cattiness and irresponsibility. Its condemnation of sexism is similarly balanced by a proclivity for victim-blaming that sits uncomfortably with early twenty-first-century, #MeToo-era gender politics. Yet, *The Craft* is a film that endures in the popular imagination (Figure 1). It speaks to the confusion and the yearning of adolescent girlhood, while also representing new possibilities for power and self-determination. While my own engagement with witchcraft was unfortunately brief, *The Craft* continues to occupy a central position in my imagination, informing my thoughts about femininity, power and friendship.

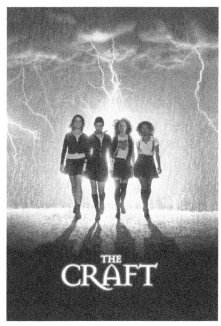

Figure 1. Promotional poster. Image: Photofest

PLOT SYNOPSIS

Released on 3 May 1996, *The Craft* was intended to be, in the words of producer Douglas Wick, about "very real teenage emotions expressed through witchcraft" (Jacobs and Brucculieri). The story begins with a typical scene of adolescent alienation and displacement, with troubled teen Sarah Bailey (Robin Tunney) uprooted from the life she had known in San Francisco and transplanted to Los Angeles with her father (Cliff DeYoung) and stepmother (Jeanine Jackson). Starting her new school, Sarah is initially alienated and overwhelmed, however she forms a brief connection with popular, charismatic football player Chris Hooker (Skeet Ulrich). Chris introduces her to the school and warns her to stay away from three strange girls – Nancy (Fairuza Balk), Bonnie (Neve Campbell) and Rochelle (Rachel True) – because they are witches. Sarah nevertheless encounters the three witches after school and accompanies them on a shopping trip to a magic shop owned by the enigmatic Lirio (Assumpta Serna). The girls

DEVIL'S ADVOCATES

bond, and after Chris spreads a cruel rumour about Sarah, they are drawn even closer together by their marginal social status. Nancy, Bonnie and Rochelle realise that Sarah possesses real power, and they bring her into their circle, or coven. United, the four teen witches grow in power and begin to use magic to improve their lives. Sarah casts a love spell on Chris; working-class Nancy uses magic to kill her abusive stepfather (John Kapelos) and improve her mother's (Helen Shaver) finances; Bonnie employs the craft to heal her disfiguring burn scars; and Rochelle curses racist bully Laura Lizzie (Christine Taylor).

During the first half of the film, the witches grow increasingly powerful, and, as they do so, their bonds deepen. They derive power from their friendship. Slowly, however, cracks begin to appear in their circle, and rivalries erode their unity. The girls' spells are also corrupted. Bonnie's newfound beauty renders her cruel and arrogant, while Rochelle starts to feel guilty when Laura Lizzie's long blonde hair falls out as a result of her curse. Sarah's love spell renders Chris dangerously obsessive and he assaults her while they are on date. Nancy grows ever more ruthless in her quest for power and begins using magic dangerously. When the girls invoke the (fictional) deity Manon, Nancy imbibes far more power than she can handle and becomes unhinged. After she discovers that Chris tried to rape Sarah, Nancy confronts him at a party and uses magic to psychically propel him out of an upstairs window to his death. Following this event, the circle disintegrates further. Sarah tries to cast a spell to bind Nancy's powers, but when the coven discovers this, they threaten Sarah and torment her with frightening visions.

Sarah seeks help from Lirio, who informs the girl that she is a natural witch, someone whose power comes from within, and that this power was likely inherited from her mother, who died in childbirth. Lirio and Sarah invoke the spirit for protection, but Sarah is frightened and flees before the spell can be completed. Sarah returns home to discover that her father and stepmother are gone. She receives a phone call from Nancy and learns that her parents have been killed in a plane crash after they mistakenly assumed that Sarah had run away to San Francisco and tried to follow her. Sarah begins to sob, and is assaulted by visions of snakes, insects and rats flooding her home. These visions harken back to Sarah's confession to the coven that she attempted suicide before she moved to Los Angeles, and that her desire to end her life was partially motivated by intrusive hallucinations featuring snakes and insects. Sarah then encounters

Rochelle, Nancy and Bonnie, who reveal that they are going to kill her and stage her death as a suicide, a punishment for her betrayal of the coven. Nancy conjures up a suicide note and slashes Sarah's wrists with a knife. With her wounds bleeding profusely, Sarah runs to hide in her bedroom where she sees a photograph of her mother come to life. Inspired by her mother's power and having discovered her own inner strength, Sarah invokes the spirit, Manon, who enables her to vanquish Rochelle and Bonnie. After a climactic battle, Sarah uses her magical prowess to defeat Nancy.

A short time later, we find Sarah happily unpacking groceries with her parents outside their sun-drenched home. Rochelle and Bonnie call to see Sarah, reassuring her that her parents' deaths were, of course, an illusion. They ask if she would like to "hang out" to practise some minor magic, and when Sarah refuses they sneer that she must have lost her powers, as they have. Sarah responds by conjuring a brief thunderstorm, compelling lightning to strike a tree branch, which falls and almost hits Rochelle and Bonnie. Sarah warns the pair that if they aren't careful they will end up like Nancy. The film cuts to a final, high-angle shot of Nancy strapped to a hospital bed. *The Craft* closes with the implication that Nancy, who abused her power, has been driven mad by it, while Sarah, who used her magic responsibly, will grow up to become a wise and powerful witch.

"CONJURING *THE CRAFT*": DEVELOPING THE FILM

The basic premise of *The Craft*, a group of social outsiders empowered by witchcraft, originated in a brainstorming session between the film's producer Douglas Wick (*Working Girl*; *Wolf*; *Girl, Interrupted*) and screenwriter Peter Filardi (*Flatliners*; *Ricky 6*). Wick was interested in collaborating with Filardi, either on a haunted house film or on a movie about adolescent witches. The teen witch plot won out because of Wick's interest in female empowerment and his fascination with how young women suddenly "come into their sexuality and have this enormous power" (Highfill, "Oral History"). In interviews, Wick and Filardi have stated that *The Craft* truly came to life after Filardi explained to Wick that "magic is historically a weapon of the underclass" and that the film's characters would need to be outsiders because "because real magic requires need" (Highfill, "Oral History"). The film was successfully pitched to Sony Studios, and while the studio was enthusiastic, *The Craft* was nevertheless an unusual project.

DEVIL'S ADVOCATES

When director and co-writer Andrew Fleming (*Threesome, Dick, Insatiable*) was brought onboard, he felt that the script recalled his own high school experience, which he describes as being a million miles away from the "pink and fun" aesthetic popularised by John Hughes in his iconic 1980s teen films (Highfill, "Oral History"). Filardi and Wick had teased out the core elements of *The Craft* between them, but Fleming developed a number of the key plot threads and fleshed out the characters. Sarah's suicide attempt, Bonnie's scarring and Rochelle's battle with racist bullies were all devised by Fleming, who drew on his own memories of high school and college for inspiration. Fleming also did a lot of research into Wicca and witchcraft, as did Filardi. Later, the production team hired Pat Devin, a practising witch and high priestess of the Covenant of the Goddess, to act as a technical adviser. According to Fleming, Devin also helped to write chants and incantations for the film, lending them an air of authenticity.

CASTING THE CIRCLE

After Fleming assumed the role of director, casting began in earnest. It took around nine months for the production team to cast Robin Tunney, Rachel True, Fairuza Balk and Nevé Campbell in the film's lead roles. During that time, casting director Pam Dixon recalls that they auditioned or met with somewhere in the region of 600 different girls and screen tested around 90 (Highfill, "Oral History"). The filmmakers also shot two scenes on film with different actresses in the four lead roles. Over the course of the casting process, the producers met with a number of actresses who would later make their mark in other roles. Angelina Jolie and Scarlett Johansson, who was only around 12 years old at the time, both read for the part of Sarah. Alicia Silverstone also tried out for the role, having just finished *Clueless*, although that film hadn't been released yet.

The first actress cast was Rachel True, who played Rochelle. Director Fleming recalls being struck not only by True's beauty, but by her capacity for humour. True herself was excited by the part of Rochelle. Although she had starred as the lead in one previous feature, she was intrigued by the possibility of a role that entailed more than the standard, somewhat limiting, position of the token Black friend. Often the parts True was offered as a woman of colour required her to simply hover on the side-lines, offering unconditional support to the white lead and bolstering their narrative, while never really having a story of her own. Fairuza Balk was, according to Fleming, the next actress cast for the film. The director and producer felt that because Nancy would be the film's nominal villain, they needed a strong actor to play the part. Balk had starred in the 1992 drama *Gas, Food, Lodging* and had received an Independent Spirit Award for her performance. No stranger to gothic fantasy, Balk had also played the role of Dorothy in the infamously dark 1985 sequel to *The Wizard of Oz*, *Return to Oz*. She also played the part of clumsy child-witch Mildred Hubble in the 1986 film adaptation of Jill Murphy's popular children's book *The Worst Witch*. Producer Douglas Wick recalls that while Balk was by no means a superstar, she was an "actor's actor", someone known and respected in the industry (Jacobs and Brucculieri). Fleming describes Balk as a practising Pagan, while Balk herself recalls that "I really did study occultism, which is very fascinating stuff" (Highfill, "Witch Rumors"). However, in a 2017 interview with *Entertainment Weekly*, Balk further clarified and dismissed rumours that she was a practising witch or Pagan. In the interview, Balk explains that she learned about the occult by visiting a magic shop in Los Angeles. Later, Balk purchased the shop, called Pan Pipes, to prevent it from being sold and turned into a Chinese restaurant. She was motivated, she claims, by a desire to preserve "the oldest occult shop in the country" (Highfill, "Witch Rumors").

Robin Tunney, who ultimately played the lead role of Sarah Bailey, initially auditioned for the role of Bonnie. In a recorded interview about the making of the film, Tunney claimed that she had always seen herself as more of a character actor and never expected to land the lead in a mainstream movie. She had recently shaved her head for the part of Debra in the comedy-drama *Empire Records* (1995), and Fleming remembers that at her audition Tunney looked like "a skinhead". She auditioned in a wig, and despite securing the role of Bonnie, the filmmakers ultimately decided that they wanted her to play Sarah, the film's lead. Tunney was initially hesitant to take on the role. She described Sarah as "boring", but her agents convinced her to take the part (Highfill, "Oral History"). The role of Bonnie eventually went to Neve Campbell, who at the time was probably the most well-known actress in the film, having completed a season of the television show *Party of Five* (1994–2000). Once the main characters were cast, Fleming shot a test scene in which the four girls strode towards the camera, decked out in vaguely witchy costumes, with a song by the band Portishead playing in the background. It was this scene, Wick claims, that ultimately led to the film being greenlit by the studio (Highfill, "Oral History"). A similar scene, in which the girls walk in slow motion with a cover of the Car's "Dangerous Type", performed by Letters to Cleo, playing in the background was used in the film and formed a central component of *The Craft*'s marketing campaign.

MAKING MAGIC: FILMING *THE CRAFT*

The Craft was filmed on location in and around Los Angeles, with many of the interiors shot on soundstages at Columbia in Culver City, a hub for film and television production since the 1910s. *The Craft*'s production designer Marek Dobrowolski has described the film as an "iconic Los Angeles piece" (Cowan), and indeed many of *The Craft*'s key scenes have a distinctly Californian or LA feel to them. Following a credit sequence consisting of a camera moving through clouds set to Our Lady Peace's cover of the Beatles' "Tomorrow Never Knows", the film opens in a rainy Los Angeles. Arriving at Los Angeles International Airport, Sarah, her father and stepmother hail a taxi in the shadow of LAX's famous Theme Building. This Space-Age structure was built in 1961 and, influenced by Populuxe and Googie architecture, resembles a flying saucer. The Theme Building is one of LA's most iconic landmarks and its presence in this scene immediately grounds the film in that city.

The torrential rain that saturates the scene here is not incidental: it was deliberately created using special effects to highlight one of *The Craft*'s central themes, the power and omnipresence of nature. Screenwriter Peter Filardi stressed that modern witchcraft is a nature-based religion, with many of its rituals centred on Aristotle's four elements – earth, air, fire and water. Each of the film's four witches embodies one of these elements. Filardi explains that Sarah, the most grounded member of the coven, is earth; Bonnie, the seer, is air; Rochelle, a competitive diver, is water; and Nancy, the most intense and driven of the witches, is fire. The credit sequence that swoops through a cloud-filled sky is suggestive of air, while the rain that soaks Sarah and her family evokes water. Later, as Sarah's family drives to their new home, they pass a snake, a creature which in Chinese astrology is associated with fire. Sarah's new home, a Spanish-style villa in Sunland, is surrounded by plants and trees, thus establishing a connection with the element of earth.

Figure 2. Rochelle, Nancy and Bonnie chanting in the gazebo. This pre-credit sequence was shot after principal photography had wrapped. The scene of the three witches chanting in the gazebo was intended to set the tone for the rest of the film. Image: Photofest

The nature motif also permeates the rest of the film (Figure 2). When Sarah arrives for her first day at St Benedict's Academy, the grounds are overgrown, covered in flowers and vines. Again, this is very much intentional. The school where many of the key scenes in *The Craft* were filmed is Verdugo Hills High School, a real school in Tujunga, LA. The building was also used in television shows like *Beverly Hills 90210* and *My So-Called Life*, as well as featuring in the 1988 film *Heathers*, a movie which many critics consider thematically similar to *The Craft*. Fleming notes that leaves and flowers were added to the school's fencing to give the impression that nature is constantly intruding on the world of the film.

The importance of nature and the four elements is also apparent in scenes where *The Craft*'s four witches work their magic. Two of the film's most important magical rituals, the initiation and the invocation of Manon, take place in natural spaces. The initiation rite was filmed beneath an oak tree in Wood Ranch, Simi Valley. According to location manager Gary Kessell, the producers wanted to shoot the scene in the accessible, nearby Griffith Park. However, as production designer Dobrowolski points out, "Griffith Park was too manicured. We really wanted a place that was untouched" (Cowan). The final Simi Valley location is shrouded in magic and mystery. It is remote, and with gentle, golden sunlight streaming through the trees, the whole area seems enchanted. The invocation of the spirit, the film's climactic ritual, also takes place in an isolated, natural space – this time at Leo Carrillo Beach, Malibu. Like many locations in and around Los Angeles, Leo Carrillo Beach has appeared in a number of films and television shows, including – somewhat ironically – light-hearted teen comedies like *Gidget* (1959) and *Beach Blanket Bingo* (1965). The isolated beach location is essential to the magic the girls work when they invoke Manon. The beach allows for views of the horizon, where the sea (water) meets the sky (air). The copious sand on the shoreline represents earth, and the girls light a bonfire, introducing the element of fire into the mix. Fleming described a number of strange incidents that occurred when they attempted to film spells or rituals outdoors. Often, the weather would change or become hostile, and filming would have to be halted. However, the beach scene was the most challenging to film. Every time the girls recited the ritual, the waves became larger and moved further up the beach. When the ritual was over the waves went back down. The crew also experienced a complete power cut during the scene where Nancy is hit by lightning. Considering the film's theme, it is hardly surprising that some crew members attributed these accidents to supernatural causes.

While location was essential to *The Craft*'s thematic engagement with the power of nature, the idea that magic is all around us is a thematic concern realised through a combination of practical and digital special effects. Andrew Fleming explains that while *The Craft* was by no means a big-budget blockbuster, Sony Imageworks – a visual effects company founded only a few years earlier – was able to create digital effects that would complement the film's aesthetic. Fleming believed that special effects in a film of this type should be carefully integrated into the movie's iconography: they should be surreal and dreamlike, but not excessive. Much of *The Craft*'s magic was achieved through practical effects. The early scene where Sarah causes a pencil to stand upright and rotate on her desk was created by running a slender metal rod through the pencil, and then placing a prop master beneath the desk to turn the rod, thus rotating the pencil. The famous "light as feather, stiff a board" scene was also created largely, although not entirely, through practical effects. The scene, which features Bonnie, Sarah and Nancy using their fingers to levitate Rochelle was not inspired by witchcraft lore, but rather by a popular slumber party game, which Fleming recalls his sister playing in their youth (Figure 3). The illusion of levitation was achieved by having actress Rachel True lie on a metallic pan affixed to a hydraulic lift. The pan was hidden by True's baggy dungarees, and the arm of the lift was later erased digitally.

Figure 3. The famous "light as a feather, stiff as a board" sequence was achieved using a combination of practical and digital effects. Image: Photofest

Other scenes made more extensive use of then-nascent CGI technology. The scene where the girls are enveloped by a cloud of butterflies following their first ritual was one of the film's most expensive shots. It involved hundreds of digitally rendered butterflies created by scanning real monarch butterflies and constructing a digital model on that basis. The scene where Sarah uses a glamour spell and changes her hair from brown to blonde was also primarily digital. Actress Robin Tunney wore a florescent green wig that acted like a green screen, allowing the effects artists to add in the colour later, transforming her hair from brown to blonde. The final confrontation between Sarah and Nancy was realised via a combination of practical and digital effects. When Nancy gives form to Sarah's worst nightmares and conjures a multitude of snakes, the filmmakers employed around 10,000 real snakes in the scene. One wide shot that depicts Sarah standing on a staircase that has been covered by a seething mass of

DEVIL'S ADVOCATES

serpents features real snakes with rubber ones placed underneath to create the illusion of depth. However, the scene in which Nancy's fingers and hair transform into snakes used CGI technology. The interweaving of subtle digital and practical effects imbues *The Craft* with a dream-like quality. The magic that permeates the film does not feel fantastical, but instead it possesses a tangible, almost tactile, veracity. The occult power harnessed by Rochelle, Nancy, Bonnie and Sarah does not appear as an esoteric mystical artform imported from some fantasy realm; rather, it feels like their magic is drawn from nature, the earth and the world around them.

"A BREW OF HAWTHORNE, 'HEATHERS' AND HOLLYWOOD HOCUS-POCUS": THE RECEPTION OF *THE CRAFT*

The Craft was released in May of 1996, and its critical reception was decidedly mixed. Critic Roger Ebert claimed that the film's failure was one of imagination. Yet, while maligning what he perceived to be a lack of creativity on the part of the filmmakers, Ebert praised the four lead actresses, enthusing that "All four are convincing performers, Balk relishes her character's loathsome behavior, and Rachel True has the sunniest smile since Doris Day". He also praised the manner in which all four play their characters as "realistic modern teenagers". The *Washington Post* was far harsher in its evaluation of *The Craft*, with critic Rita Kempley complaining about the film's messy structure and derivative plot. Her review dismissed the film as a "brew of Hawthorne, 'Heathers' and Hollywood hocus-pocus". Clearly intended as criticism, Kempley's review nevertheless touched on one of the most fascinating aspects of *The Craft*: the intriguing manner in which it fuses the kind of American witchcraft lore found in the work of nineteenth-century author Nathaniel Hawthorne with the dark high school comedy perfected by *Heathers*. Other critical responses to *The Craft* were kinder. The *San Francisco Chronicle* described *The Craft* as "the smartest and most satisfying horror thriller to come out in a while". Lauding the emotional impact of the film, the *Chronicle* review suggested that *The Craft*'s power resides primarily in how it "recognizes that the emotions set loose in high school are of the most fierce variety".

Much of the negative response to *The Craft*, however, seems to have been grounded in a failure to understand the film's intended audience. Andrew Fleming has claimed

THE CRAFT

that he wanted the film to be a PG13. Indeed, the film does not feature excessive gore or nudity, and employs the word "fuck" only once, in a non-sexual context, in order to adhere to MPAA guidelines for the awarding of a PG13 rating. Peter Filardi stressed in interviews that *The Craft* was "designed for 16-, 15-, 14-year-olds" (Jacobs and Brucculieri), but the MPAA ultimately awarded it an R-rating, meaning that those under 17 could not view the film without parental accompaniment. According to Fleming, the MPAA determined that *The Craft* deserved an R-rating because it featured teenagers practising "black magic". This undoubtedly impacted *The Craft*'s critical reception, as the higher rating encouraged many critics to treat the film as a work produced for adults rather than young teenagers. The misapprehension that *The Craft* was created as a mature horror film intended for an adult audience led many critics to denounce the film as a failure.

In a *HitFix* interview recorded in 2016, Douglas Wick suggests that *The Craft* may just have been ahead of its time. For Wick, *The Craft* was "YA before YA", a film that spoke authentically about teenage emotions and issues in a heightened genre (Eggersten). While young adult fiction has been around for a long time, with the Young Adult Services Division of the American Library Association being founded in 1957, the genre really exploded in the late 1990s and early 2000s. Following the success of the Harry Potter series, *Twilight* and *The Hunger Games*, the notion that fantasy or science fiction aimed at young people, between the ages of 12 and 18, could be both creative and lucrative, has become an accepted part of contemporary cultural discourse. *The Craft*, however, was released just before the YA publishing boom, and so, many critics and audience members simply didn't know what to do with it. As Fleming states in the same interview, *The Craft* was produced during a "weird moment in pop culture when teen movies were all kind of John Hughes, pink and cheery". *The Craft* simply didn't reflect the aesthetic or the kind of thematic concerns that characterised teen films of the period: questions of popularity are supplanted by more unsettling concerns with racist bullying; makeovers involve the healing of disfiguring scars; and the fashion is decidedly gothic in style. *The Craft*'s status as a sort of proto-YA text can also be observed in its immediate and enduring popularity amongst teenagers and young women. Interviewed following the film's initial box-office success – it opened at number one in North America and made an estimated $7 million during its opening weekend – Jeff Blake, head of Sony

13

Pictures/Columbia's distribution, attributed *The Craft*'s success to teenagers and young women: "The teenagers loved it because it was their movie and young women went for it because the sub-theme is about women taking control" (Brennan). Likewise, while *The Craft*'s overall box office returns only reached about $55.6 million, the film was highly successful on VHS, becoming a popular rental and a staple of slumber parties throughout the late 1990s and early 2000s.

READING *THE CRAFT*

In the three chapters that follow, this book frames *The Craft* as a cinematic exploration of adolescence and frames its use of witchcraft as an extended metaphor for the teenage experience. The first chapter attempts to situate *The Craft* within the broader context of the 1990s, exploring how the film's central themes reflect the key social, political and cultural concerns of the decade. This chapter also locates *The Craft* within the cinematic context of the 1990s. Here, I connect *The Craft* to what Alexandra West calls the "1990s Teen Horror Cycle", a series of films that transformed the pre-millennial cinematic landscape. I also place the film within the broader history of American teen cinema. The second chapter reads *The Craft* as a film about witches and investigates its connection to both historical and pop cultural representations of witchcraft. Chapter 2 explores how *The Craft* draws on and subverts the early modern stereotype of the Satanic witch, while also engaging with 1980s/1990s fears about teen Satanism. This chapter contextualises *The Craft* within a lengthy, often complex, history of cinematic witches that stretches all the way back to the silent era. The third chapter analyses *The Craft*'s engagement with social issues, including gender, sexuality, harassment and racism. Reading the film through the lens of both postfeminist ideology and the third-wave feminist movement that was contemporary with its release, this chapter argues that *The Craft*'s treatment of sexual assault, systemic racism and economic inequality reflects debates and discourses that were prevalent in the media, on college campuses and amongst activists at the time. In the book's conclusion, I provide a brief overview of *The Craft*'s legacy, from its impact on subsequent television shows and movies (like *Buffy the Vampire Slayer* and *Charmed*) through to its role in reviving popular interest in witchcraft, particularly amongst the young.

THE CRAFT

Throughout this book, my analysis remains thematic rather than aesthetic in its focus. Influenced by Catherine Driscoll's research on teen cinema, I believe that, in the case of many films aimed at this demographic, their commentary on adolescence, what they have to say about the teenage experience, generally eclipses their formal conventions. Such films rarely endeavour to break new ground in terms of editing or *mise en scène*. However, they are often pioneering in how they treat social and cultural issues relevant to their teenage audience. In her work on the cinema of adolescence, Driscoll is careful to note that "Teen film is generally thought more interesting for what it says about youth than for any aesthetic innovations, and is represented as closely tied to the historically changing experience of adolescence" (2). Likewise, this study of *The Craft* largely eschews discussion of its directorial or editing styles in favour of a focus on its context, characters and themes. Like many fans of *The Craft*, my interest lies in how the film treats adolescence and what it has to say about the uniquely tumultuous, disconcerting experience of teenage girlhood. I am fascinated with its use of witchcraft, its subversion of mystical iconography and its creative use of the occult as a metaphor for growing up. In the pages that follow, I hope to show that *The Craft* is not simply about the magic of spells and glamorous transformations, but that it is a film intimately bound up with the strange, often frightening magic of teenage girlhood.

CHAPTER 1: FROM REAGANISM TO RIOTS: SITUATING *THE CRAFT* IN THE 1990S

Positioned at the tail-end of the last century, the 1990s was a decade of tumult and transformation. The nineties in America were ushered in by a change of leadership when icon of 1980s conservatism Ronald Regan was succeeded by his vice-president George W. Bush in 1989 and by Democrat Bill Clinton in 1993. Regan's vision for the 1980s was characterised by a clear agenda based on "the three Ps, prosperity, patriotism, and peace" (Troy 18). Consequently, it had been an era defined by reactionary politics, appeals to traditionalism and the fetishisation of affluence. As the decade turned, a number of the political structures and cultural paradigms that had ordered American culture for much of the past half-century collapsed. The East/West divide that separated the Communism of Eastern Europe from the democratic capitalism of Western Europe and the United States began to dissolve when the Berlin Wall fell in 1989, and by 1991 the Soviet Union ceased to exist entirely. The Cold War that had split the globe in two for almost five decades had come to an end rather suddenly and without the apocalyptic nuclear conflict that many assumed would be its inevitable culmination. The USSR, America's long-time enemy, had retreated, and the 1990s began with the United States lacking a definite, sufficiently nefarious foreign adversary. As the decade advanced, however, a number of domestic terrorist attacks, including a bomb blast at the World Trade Centre in 1993 and the Oklahoma City bombing in 1995, raised the grim possibility that America's enemies were no longer recognisably foreign or safely external. The United States now had to grapple with the reality of enemies within its borders.

The dawn of the 1990s witnessed an explosion of economic strife. The United States lost between 300,000 and 1 million manufacturing jobs under the Regan administration, and, consequently, the average wage for ordinary American families declined sharply in the early years of the decade (Muir 5). Outlining the impact of this economic downturn on the American population, Christina Lee observes that the world-weary cynicism often viewed as characteristic of nineties youth was shaped by serious economic recessions in both the early eighties and the very early nineties (20). Here, Lee draws attention to the harsh fact that the so-called "Generation-X", young people born between the early 1960s and the early 1980s, were destined to be less financially successful than, or at the very best on a par with, their parents (21). Raised with the high expectations of mothers and fathers who had come of age in the affluent post-war years, members of Generation-X had grown up to believe that they too would slip easily into successful careers and acquire comfortable homes in dreamy suburbs. However, by the early 1990s, it was readily apparent that Gen-Xers would never experience the prosperity enjoyed by their parents' generation.

Nevertheless, despite the general air of pessimism that defined the first years of the decade, the American economy had more or less recovered by the mid-1990s and continued to expand as the new millennium approached. Indeed, as early as 1993, the economy was already displaying signs of improvement, with the creation of 3.3 million new jobs (Troy 111). Describing the accelerated pace of America's economic expansion during the mid-1990s, the historian Haynes Johnson describes how,

> Driven by the force of the longest, continuous peacetime boom, the expanding American economy lifted what was already the highest standard of living in the world to even greater heights. So rapid was the growth, so sustained the boom, that Americans were experiencing the best of all economic worlds: low inflation and low unemployment, high productivity and record high profits. (qtd. in Muir 8–9)

In this way, the American nineties were characterised by two seemingly contradictory moods: a cynicism crystallised by the malaise of the decade's early years and a growing complacency that expanded as economic growth accelerated in the latter part of the decade.

A similar schism defined the political arena of the 1990s, as an ever-widening gulf between social and political ideologies further polarised American life. After the apparent conservative consensus of the Reagan era, the nineties witnessed a pronounced and very public split between conservative and liberal attitudes towards abortion and reproductive rights, gun control, LGBTQ+ rights, the role of women in public life and recreational drugs. During the 1992 Republican Primary, the conservative columnist and commentator Pat Buchanan famously described the ideological split that was beginning to shape modern American life as a "culture war". Although the term did not originate with Buchanan, his speech highlighted the stark division between the Clinton agenda – characterised by what he called "abortion on demand" and gay rights – and the conservative traditionalism of Bush and the Reaganite legacy. Painting

THE CRAFT

this split as a decisive moment that would determine the future of America, Buchanan framed the rift between Republicans and Democrats as "a cultural war, as critical to the kind of nation we will one day be as was the Cold War itself" (qtd. in Muir 6). After the election of Bill Clinton in 1992, these divisions deepened, and while many conservatives had speculated that Clinton's victory would usher in a triumphant liberal agenda, his presidency only served to exacerbate existing conflicts. In 1993, the Clinton administration approved the notorious "Don't ask, don't tell" policy that enabled gay men and women to serve in the US military, as long as they did not disclose their sexual orientation. This policy, with its enforced closeting, failed to appeal to liberals and also disappointed conservatives, who had advocated a complete ban on gays in the armed services (Troy 80). Later, in 1996, Clinton signed the Defense of Marriage Act (DOMA), a law that defined marriage as a union between one man and one woman, and empowered states to refuse recognition of same-sex marriages.

America in the 1990s was a nation divided, and *The Craft* (1996) is a film both informed by and reflective of this cultural division. While clearly straining towards progressive, even empowering, ideas about femininity and sex, it nevertheless falls back on regressive stereotypes and a punitive attitude towards sexuality. At the same time, it appears caught between the fervent consumerism that emerged in the mid-nineties and the cynicism so often viewed as characteristic of Generation X. The girls who form the witches' coven at the heart of the film are torn between embracing their outsider status – revelling in their position as the school freaks – and their desire for the signifiers of nineties consumerist excess, conventional beauty and high-status heteronormative relationships. There is a conflict running throughout *The Craft* that not only heightens the tensions at the centre of the film but also exposes the conflicts and contradictions inherent to American society in the 1990s. In this way, *The Craft* sits comfortably within the broader corpus of nineties teen horror cinema. As Alexandra West notes in her groundbreaking study of 1990s horror, "The central conflict and tension within the 1990s Teen Horror Cycle is between the generation coming of age and the choices of their parents" (11). As West goes on to explain, films of this period are marked by a profound schism between complacency of the Baby Boomers and the cynicism of their Gen X children, a theme that is often expressed thematically by the failure of parents to protect their children from danger (11).

19

DEVIL'S ADVOCATES

THE DARK SIDE OF THE 1990s: RACISM AND VIOLENCE IN LOS ANGELES

The duality at the core of *The Craft* emerges as a theme early in the film and is perhaps most immediately apparent in the film's setting. Following an opening credit sequence in which the camera appears to float through a cloud-filled sky, we touch down in Los Angeles. This, however, is not the LA of sunshine and Hollywood glamour. Our first glimpse of the city is obscured by rain, as torrents of water pour down on Los Angeles International Airport (LAX). Although difficult to shoot in, director Andrew Fleming has stressed that the location was chosen because it is one of the few iconic, locatable landmarks in Los Angeles. The famous 1960s Googie-style architecture, so emblematic of LAX and so often a welcoming sight for would-be stars emerging from the airport into the bright California sunshine, appears here as a grey, washed-out monument to disillusionment. As Sarah and her family load their luggage into a taxi, the grey skies behind them promise only despondency. Having moved from San Francisco to LA with the intention of starting over following the troubled Sarah's suicide attempt, the dream of a happy home in Southern California appears to have already evaporated.

When Sarah, along with her father and stepmother, arrives at her new home, a palatial Spanish-style villa, chosen by the production team for its power to evoke the lost world of old Hollywood, the house is dark and rain leaks through the ceiling. In one of the film's few jump scares, Sarah's unpacking is disturbed by a homeless man who has wandered into their property with a snake in his hands. Although clearly intended to establish Sarah's fear of snakes, the appearance of the homeless man also speaks to the degradation of Los Angeles, its poverty, and the immense economic gulf between the city's disenfranchised and affluent upper-middle-class families, like Sarah's. In a 2016 interview with the *Guardian* newspaper, director Andrew Fleming articulates the duality inherent in the city: "I grew up in Los Angeles and always found it such a peculiar place. You have this glossy city, the LA most people think of, but there's this whole other side to it: eerie, mysterious, almost gothic. That's what I wanted *The Craft* to be like".

When Sarah first agrees to spend time with teen witches Rochelle, Nancy and Bonnie, their inaugural group outing is to an impoverished section of downtown Los Angeles. According to assistant location manager Brett Williams, "Back then it was bad [*downtown*]. It was shady as hell. You didn't want to be down there at night" (Cowan). Lit by neon and cluttered with rundown storefronts, the underbelly of the city speaks again to the divisions inherent in American life at the time. Aside from the decidedly working-class Nancy, the other girls are merely tourists, middle-class day-trippers for whom an excursion into the city's seedy underside constitutes a thrilling act of rebellion. Production designer Marek Dobrowolski emphasises this sense of socio-economic division in an interview with *LA Weekly*: "You had all those theaters that were turned into Hispanic shops. It had a great foreign vibe. It was like a forgotten world, with the homeless people mingling with drug addicts. [...] It was like a forbidden land for girls from the [wealthier San Fernando] Valley (Cowan). The contrast between the homes occupied by most of the girls, as well as their seemingly affluent private school, and the decaying downtown highlights the socio-economic disparity that defined American life at the time and appeared especially stark in cities like Los Angeles (Figure 4).

Figure 4. The witches visit downtown Los Angeles. Image: Photofest

By the mid-1990s, Los Angeles had emerged as an emblem of the divisions and conflicts that threatened to tear America in two. In March of 1991, a 25-year-old African American man named Rodney King was detained by the LAPD for speeding and was violently beaten by a number of police officers. The incident was captured on camcorder, and once it fell into the hands of the media, it was played repeatedly on major American news networks. Despite the exposure the incident received, the officers were acquitted on charges of using excessive force in April 1992. Outrage over this verdict engulfed the city, and the resulting violence constituted what has been described as the "worst civilian riot in American history" (Muir 35). Almost 4,000 buildings were vandalised, businesses burned and 53 people lost their lives. As Gil Troy notes in his study of American culture in the 1990s, the beating of Rodney King and the riots that followed the acquittal of the perpetrators exposed the pervasive, but largely repressed, racial divisions that continued to shape American society (34).

By the 1990s, many Americans wanted to believe that they had transcended the monstrous racism of previous decades and centuries. Yet, as Troy observes, racial inequality had never disappeared, and by the nineties the economic consequences of institutional racism were apparent in the troubling fact that while the child poverty rate for white Americans was 15 per cent, it was as high as 39 per cent for Hispanics and 45 per cent for African Americans (34). When the Los Angeles riots ignited in 1992, the fury that propelled their violence stemmed from decades of mounting racial tensions and an awareness of the oppressive systems that continued to disenfranchise people of colour. When rioters took to the streets of LA, their battle cry was "LAPD ARE REDNECKS! LAPD ARE RACISTS!" (Troy 63). For many African Americans, the riots were an opportunity to fight back against a justice system that unfairly profiled, interrogated and intimidated them.

Questions of race and racism are both implicit and explicit in *The Craft*, and they will be explored more fully in Chapter 3. In its most overt form, the racism that haunted American life during the ostensibly progressive nineties is visible in the bullying endured by Rochelle, the only Black member of the coven. The popular Laura Lizzie torments Rochelle largely by mocking her African American features, particularly her hair, and the intensity of this bullying highlights the persistence of racist attitudes into the latter part of the last millennium. At the same time, Laura's tendency to attack Rochelle's failure to conform to a dominant, Eurocentric aesthetic also indicates how American racism had become more insidious as the century progressed. Rather than manifesting in explicitly racist laws, such as enforced segregation, racist attitudes instead colonised cultural spaces in more subtle ways by designating darker skin and natural hair inferior to European features, light skin and silky, straight hair.

Figure 5. The Virgin of Guadalupe (Virgen de Guadalupe) *by Manuel de Arellano (1691). Image: Public domain*

The entrenchment of racist social structures can also be seen in the film's Los Angeles setting. Although segregated along economic lines – the girls' excursion into the "scary", impoverished downtown perfectly encapsulates this division – the city is also divided along racial and ethnic lines. Los Angeles is, in reality, an extremely diverse city, with a large Hispanic population that continued to expand in the 1990s. However, for much of the film this diversity is absent. Rochelle is the only character of colour to speak in *The Craft*, and while Hispanic and Asian students can be seen in the backgrounds of scenes that take place in the girls' high school, none of them is named, nor do they speak. The script does describe Lirio, the magic shop owner as "Latina", but Assumpta Serna (the actress who plays Lirio) is Catalonian, and the character's ethnicity remains ambiguous. In many ways, the marginalisation of people of colour in *The Craft* is indicative of cinematic and televisual norms at the time. In the early and mid-nineties, a significant proportion of mainstream films and television shows remained overwhelmingly white, with people of colour only appearing as background characters, tokens, or during very special episodes that explicitly tackled issues of racism.

DEVIL'S ADVOCATES

The Craft does, however, make numerous visual references to Los Angeles' Hispanic community and their presence within the city. When Rochelle, Nancy, Bonnie and Sarah first venture downtown to visit the magic shop, they pass a mural – created specifically by the film's production team – that is decorated with Hispanic artistic motifs. Immense and colourful, the mural dwarfs the girls and appears to swallow them up. At an earlier point in the film, Sarah is discussing Nancy and the other witches with her love interest, Chris, and when the camera turns towards the girls, they are framed by a massive, colourful mural of the Virgin of Guadalupe – also created specifically for the film. This wide shot of the girls sitting beneath the brilliant mural was the first scene filmed for *The Craft,* and the positioning of the teen witches in relation to the Virgin Mary appears laden with meaning.

An icon of Mexican Catholicism, the Virgin of Guadalupe (Figure 5) is said to embody the characteristics of a pre-Columbian deity, the Earth Mother Tonantzin, to whom offerings were made on the hill of Tepeyac centuries before the arrival of Spanish colonisers (Alvarez Sesma). Framing the coven beneath the vibrant image of this syncretic figure – at once an emblem of Mexican Catholicism and a remnant of a pre-Christian goddess – anticipates the feminine supernatural power that the young witches will later embody. However, it also gestures towards an omnipresent yet invisible Hispanic presence. The overwhelmingly white Los Angeles the girls inhabit is one in which they rarely interact with the city's immense Hispanic community, yet it is a city pervaded by traces of this community. That such traces and gestures towards the Hispanic community are apparent while the community itself remains invisible again suggests a city and a nation divided along racial lines.

As well as touching upon racial divisions, *The Craft* also foregrounds the duality of adolescent life in the 1990s. While many of the teenagers who attend the Catholic, presumably private, high school where much of the film takes place are wealthy – they drive expensive cars and hold parties in palatial homes – there is also a sense that danger pervades the adolescent experience. The working-class Nancy is abused by her violent stepfather, Rochelle is the victim of racist bullying, and Sarah is almost raped by a classmate. Moreover, the school environment itself seems fraught with danger. Early in the film, when Rochelle, Nancy and Bonnie are discussing the arrival of a fourth witch to complete their circle, Nancy fixes her gaze on a middle-aged, female security guard and sarcastically suggests, "Maybe she could be our fourth". Although constituting a brief, throw-away joke, the presence of this security guard on campus, combined with a later scene featuring a male security guard meandering through lunch tables in the background of a shot, indicates an intense paranoia about school safety.

These sequences are indicative of the widespread concern with school safety that emerged during this period. The 1990s, after all, witnessed the introduction of metal detectors and armed security personnel to American schools. This even appears as a gag in the contemporary teen romance *Never Been Kissed* (1999), when investigative journalist Josie Geller (Drew Barrymore) returns to high school and is shocked to see security guards on patrol and students filing through metal detectors on their way to class. In his study of nineties horror cinema, John Kenneth Muir claims that the 1990s was defined by a "strange pattern of school-related violence", ranging from gun crime to sexual assault (38). One example cited by Muir is the prominent case of eight high school athletes arrested in March 1993 in Lakewood, California. Nicknamed the "Spur Posse", the boys had been engaged in an elaborate game whereby they accrued points by having sex with female students, "scoring" whether the girls slept with them of their own free will or acquiesced out of fear (39). The Spur Posse became infamous in the 1990s not only because of the perversity of their "game", but also because of how these popular, affluent young men were defended by their community. The event would later inspire Kat Shea's 1999 film *The Rage: Carrie II*, but it also seems to have influenced aspects of *The Craft*. Sarah's relationship with Chris Hooker undoubtedly evokes this incident, with Chris not only spreading rumours about bedding Sarah, but later trying to rape her while under the influence of a love spell.

At the same time, there were around 25 school shootings in the United States between 1990 and 1999. It is no wonder, then, that films like *The Craft* would depict high school environments that were constantly under the watchful eye of law enforcement. The nineties was a decade in which violence and death had infiltrated formerly safe spaces. Concomitantly, the film's representation of teenage girls as monsters, or more specifically witches, also chimes with the cultural discourse of an era defined by school-centred violence. In cases like that of the Spur Posse, as well as in many of the school shootings that took place during the 1990s, the perpetrators were not outsiders, unknown and sinister strangers; rather, they were teenagers who were themselves part of the school community. This fear of internal violence also manifested in films of the period. As West explains, "The 1990s teen horror films situated the terror in America's backyards, communities and families. [...] The antagonists in the 1990s were friends and family members [...] Horror had truly come home" (9). Similarly, in *The Craft* we see numerous instances of intra-group violence. Teenagers engage in racist bullying, high school boys assault their female classmates, and, as the film progresses, a group of teenage witches enacts often violent revenge on their peers. The violence that pervades the high school environment does not come from without and is not usually perpetrated by adults. Instead, *The Craft*, mirroring contemporary fears about school violence, portrays teenagers turning on and harming each other.

"REVIVING OPHELIA": TEENAGE GIRLS IN THE 1990S

Although director Andrew Fleming claims to have drawn heavily on his own high school memories in making *The Craft*, the film is nevertheless firmly enmeshed in the youth culture of the 1990s. Screenwriter Peter Filardi recalls immersing himself in the angst-ridden music of the era's grunge and Riot Grrrl movements, remarking that "Hole's 'Live Through This' was spot-on for me musically while writing 'The Craft.' It's that raw power of adolescent pain. I still think of 'The Craft' whenever I hear 'Doll Parts' or 'Softer Softest'" (Jacobs and Brucculieri). The influence of bands like Hole (a group fronted by grunge-era icon Courtney Love) is palpable throughout *The Craft*, as the film not only revels in the messy, grungy aesthetic of the period, but also reflects the cynical disillusionment of nineties youth culture. For many, this was an era symbolised by the increased visibility of Generation-X, young people coming of age in the early and mid-nineties who rejected the optimism of their Baby Boomer parents (see above). Yet, while *The Craft* is saturated by the rebellious, disaffected spirit of this period, the film remains notable for its focus on the experiences of young women. This, of course, is natural for a film centred on witchcraft, a topic that often serves as an area of intrigue for teenage girls. At the same time, *The Craft* was a response to changing viewer demographics, with an increasing number of young women attending the cinema in the 1990s.

In the introduction to their book *Sugar, Spice, and Everything Nice: Cinemas of Girlhood*, Frances Gateward and Murray Pomerance discuss how, from the perspective of

THE CRAFT

television and movie studios, teenage girls were becoming an increasingly important demographic during the 1990s and early 2000s. Gateward and Pomerance note that, according to Teenage Research Unlimited, teens during this period spent an average of $153 billion per annum on entertainment and consumer goods, with adolescent girls spending an average of $91 a week (15). While their male counterparts spent their money on video games and sports, young women preferred shopping and going to the movies (15). In the 1980s and 1990s, as small neighbourhood theatres were replaced by large multiplexes, usually located in shopping malls, these two activities merged and became inextricably linked in the minds of young girls, who would supplement shopping trips with group cinema excursions. Gateward and Pomerance also identify a thematic shift taking place in the cinema of this period, with popular films moving away from the concerns of young men and towards the interests of teen girls. This trend began with the success of Amy Heckerling's 1995 film *Clueless* and continued with movies like *Romeo + Juliet* (1996), *The Opposite of Sex* (1998), *She's All That* (1998) and *Dick* (1999; also directed by Andrew Fleming) (15–16). Similarly, Alexandra West observes that the new wave of nineties teen slashers, including *Scream* (1996), *I Know What You Did Last Summer* (1997) and *Urban Legend* (1998) placed a greater emphasis on the final girl (the film's triumphant heroine) as an enduring, consistent point of audience identification.

The teen girl film was so pervasive in the mid-nineties that writer Peggy Orenstein suggested 1996 be christened "the year of the teen-age girl". For Orenstein, girl culture was everywhere in the 1990s, from Alanis Morissette concerts where "thousands of ululating 13-year-olds […] thrill to her hit 'Ironic'" to the popular series *My So-Called Life*, "a drama about a 15-year-old girl and her angst [that] plays in perpetual reruns on MTV". Alongside these expressions of teen angst, Orenstein also cites the ubiquity of films for and about teenage girls in American cinemas during the mid-nineties. Orenstein distinguishes these 1990s teen films from their predecessors because of the agency they afford to their female protagonists. She describes these works as

> Films […] in which girls are in charge of their own fates, active rather than reactive; films that are about girls' relationships to one another rather than to boys, that tackle the big themes of teen-age life, like anger, sexuality, alienation and displacement.

27

As with many of these films, *The Craft* reflects the concerns of teen girls in the 1990s as well as providing them with aspirational images of power and strength. Its heroines are active, seeking power for themselves while simultaneously navigating complex questions of sexuality, identity and purpose.

However, while *The Craft*'s protagonists are afforded a great deal of individual agency, the film nevertheless draws on contemporary ideas about female adolescents as uniquely troubled, lost and wayward. Although reflecting a wide array of then-current discourses, many of these ideas about young women were influenced by popular non-fiction books such as Mary Pipher's *Reviving Ophelia: Saving the Selves of Adolescent Girls* (1994). *Reviving Ophelia* was based on Pipher's work with the teen girls she encountered in her therapy practice. Many of them struggled with serious problems – suicidal ideation, teenage pregnancy and eating disorders – while others faced comparatively minor issues like moodiness and conflict with parents and other authority figures. In her book, Pipher queries why girls in the 1990s experienced more difficulty navigating adolescence than she and her friends did in the early sixties. Pipher wonders why, despite all the advances made by the women's movement, modern girl culture seemed defined by misery and oppression. Ultimately, Pipher blames the escalation of depression, eating disorders, self-harm and promiscuity on contemporary media culture with its relentless expectations of beauty and sexual availability. Describing nineties culture as a "girl-poisoning culture", Pipher argues that modern adolescent unhappiness derives largely from ubiquitous media messages that demand young women meet impossible standards of beauty and sexual allure (12). Similarly, the emergence of popular postfeminist ideologies functioned as what Angela McRobbie terms a "double entanglement", treating feminism as a movement that has "passed away", its goals achieved, while at the same time replicating regressive ideas about women's bodies and lives (12). The nineties also witnessed a proliferation of new media ranging from intrusive tabloid magazines to the nascent information superhighway and the beginning of 24-hour cable news programming. According to Pipher, the pervasiveness of popular media in the lives of young women creates a sort of "second parent", popular culture, who imparts upon them the importance of fame and glamour and teaches them that their bodies are objects to be gazed upon and enjoyed by others. Consequently, Pipher explains, girls become fragmented during adolescence, "their selves split into mysterious contradictions" (20).

It is for this reason that, according to the Centre for Disease Control, the suicide rate amongst 10- to 14-year-olds rose 75 per cent between 1979 and 1988 (Pipher 27).

The Craft engages with this notion of female adolescence as a difficult period marked by social pressures, familial strife and psychological tumult. Suicide and self-harm are ubiquitous throughout the film. One of the first pieces of biographical information we learn about Sarah is that she attempted suicide before her family relocated to Los Angeles. When she shares this information with the coven, Bonnie looks at the scars emblazoned on Sarah's wrists and informs her that she "even did it the right way", cutting vertically rather than horizontally. Bonnie's knowledge of the correct method for slitting one's wrists suggests that she too has either attempted suicide or given serious consideration to ending her life. The casual nature of their conversation and Rochelle's almost humorous attempt to find how exactly Bonnie knows so much about the subject suggests that suicide and self-harm, rather than being shockingly anomalous, have become common, almost mundane, aspects of girl culture in the late twentieth century.

Not only does Sarah engage in self-harm, but she also experiences a violent sexual assault. She is almost raped by her high school crush Chris while he is under a love spell. That Sarah is presented as implicitly responsible for Chris's actions by virtue of the magical enchantment she casts over him is one of the more troubling aspects of a film that is generally rather progressive in its depiction of gender and sexuality. However, when combined with the sexual double standard that pervades the high school – girls like Nancy are viewed as "sluts" for engaging in sexual activities, while men like Chris are celebrated for their prowess – the film's approach to the subject of sexual violence can be seen as indicative of the complex sexual arena that many young people had to navigate at the time. More liberal attitudes towards sex and greater access to contraception meant that more high school students were sexually active than ever before. Nevertheless, misogynistic ideas about female sexuality persisted, and abstinence-only sex education, which was becoming prevalent in many states during the 1990s, helped to reinforce these ideas. In *Reviving Ophelia*, Pipher discusses a study carried out amongst teenagers in the state of Rhode Island. In response to a question that asked when, if ever, a man has the right to force a woman to have sex with him, 80 per cent said that the man has the right to use force if the couple is married, 70 per cent said that force was justified if they planned to marry, while 61 per cent said it was acceptable if a couple had had prior sexual relations. More than half said that "force" was warranted if the woman had "led him on", and 30 per cent said force was justified if he knew she had had sex with other men (206). The complex and often contradictory attitudes towards sexuality displayed in *The Craft* are, therefore, reflective of the confusion felt by many adolescent girls in the early and mid-nineties. Inhabiting a more liberalised sexual arena, and plagued by the cultural expectation that young women should be sexual beings, they were also painfully aware that their sexuality was subject to social control and would be punished if it was deemed excessive or threatening. (See Chapter 3 for more on this.)

THE CINEMATIC CONTEXT OF *THE CRAFT*

The Craft is a film that takes seriously the anxieties of teenage girls. Its attitude to adolescent femininity is neither exploitative nor condescending, and it is this emphasis on the emotional lives of adolescent girls that distinguishes *The Craft* from many earlier teen horror films. Horror movies produced for an adolescent market in previous decades often relied on stereotypical characters and situations in order to moralise about promiscuity and irresponsible behaviour. As Muir explains,

> After the conservative Reagan Revolution of 1980, the popular "slasher" or "dead teenager" movie quickly became the most popular of all horror movie plots, showcasing an Old Testament-style response to sin and the "do whatever feels good," counter-culture aesthetic of the late 1960s and early 1970s. (4)

Muir defines this as the "vice precedes slice and dice paradigm" (4) and observes how such films reduce the complex world of adolescence to a decadent obsession with sex, alcohol and drugs, an obsession which must be invariably punished in order to maintain the moral status quo. *The Craft*, while clearly influenced by earlier horror cinema, is nevertheless a product of the nineties, shaped less by the staunch conservatism of the Regan era and more by the conflicts the 1990s culture wars. It is a film that strains towards progressivism and empowerment, while at the same time, falling back on more regressive ideas about gender and sexuality. In its conflicted, and sometimes contradictory, approach to issues such as sex, race and class, *The Craft* is very much a product of its time, reflecting the changing attitudes of nineties America and the double bind of postfeminist ideology.

The Craft has much in common with what Alexandra West terms the "1990s Teen Horror Cycle" (see above), a series of films that began with Fran Rubel Kuzui's *Buffy the Vampire Slayer* in 1992 and ended with Geoffrey Wright's *Cherry Falls* in 2000. These nineties horror films, while drawing on elements of their predecessors – particularly the violent slashers of the late seventies and eighties – were distinguished by their cynical wit, self-reflexivity and postmodern referentiality. West identifies films such as *Fear* (1996), *Scream*, *I Know What You Did Last Summer*, *Urban Legend* and *The Faculty* (1998) as key components of this rejuvenated youth horror cycle. Although popular with multiplex-going adolescents, many older horror fans were dismissive of these glossier, youth-friendly films. As West notes, "To many horror fans the 1990s Teen Horror Cycle took what was once an underground movement and made it palatable for the masses while ignoring the elements that made these films of the 1970s and 1980s unique" (9). Certainly, many of the films lacked the visual or cinematic innovation of their seventies predecessors, with few nineties slashers attaining anything close to the striking, sun-drenched cinematography of *The Texas Chain Saw Massacre* (1974) or the ambitious extend POV shot that opens *Halloween* (1978). Nevertheless, nineties teen slashers often managed to excel in their characterisation and witty dialogue. Moreover, films of this period were defined not just by their debt to a pre-existing body of horror cinema, but also by their reliance on conventions derived from popular teen comedies and romance films, like *Sixteen Candles* (1984) and *Pretty in Pink* (1986). Horror movies of the 1990s are unique, then, because they draw with equal enthusiasm on the films of John Carpenter and John Hughes. *The Craft*, like many of its nineties contemporaries, is as much a film about teenagers and high school as it is a film about violence, the occult and terror.

While films about teenagers have existed for almost as long as the cinematic medium itself, youth cinema really exploded during the post-Second World War era. In the United States, the post-war economic boom enabled young people to stay in school longer, extending the transitional period between childhood and adulthood. With more time spent in school, teenagers began to turn to their classmates rather than to their families or communities for support and guidance. They created peer groups centred around shared musical tastes, hobbies and fashions. As Timothy Shary explains,

DEVIL'S ADVOCATES

Other factors contributed to the burgeoning presence of the teenager in the 1950s: the greater availability of automobiles, which allowed youth to travel and thus achieve a certain independence; the recovering economy, which gave many teens extra money for entertainment outside the home; the popular reception of rock and roll music, which clearly flew in the face of previous standards; and the influence of television, which, while giving all Americans a new common entertainment medium, also kept more adults at home. (3–4)

While the immediate post-war period saw a number of so-called "clean teen" performances in comparatively wholesome youth films such as *Margie* (1946), *A Date with Judy* (1948) and *Little Women* (1949), the 1950s saw the arrival of more subversive teen films like *The Wild One* (1953) and *Rebel Without a Cause* (1955) (Shary 4). These works depicted troubled teenagers who fought with their parents, stayed out late and drove fast cars. In doing so, they showed that adolescence was not merely an extension of childhood or a training ground for responsible adulthood, but rather an emotionally turbulent period during which young people attempted to carve out their own identities, separate from their parents and families. Such films not only reflected the adolescent experience, they also functioned as an imaginative arena where teenagers could themselves negotiate aspects of their own identities and figure out what it meant to be a teen.

As the twentieth century progressed and neighbourhood cinemas were replaced by multiplexes that inhabited the top tiers of shopping malls, teenagers were lured to the movies not just by the content of the films that played, but by the location of the theatres themselves. Ensconced between fast food restaurants and clothing stores, the multiplex became a central facet of the teenage experience. From the 1980s onwards, the relocation of cinemas to shopping malls also made it apparent to Hollywood studios that their core demographic was now made up of the teens who frequented those malls and "formed the first generation of multiplex moviegoers" (Shary 6). Teen films proliferated during the 1980s, encompassing everything from slashers (*Friday the 13th* [1980], *A Nightmare on Elm Street* [1984]) and science fiction movies (*War Games* [1983], *Weird Science* [1985]) to romance (*Sixteen Candles*), and even dark comedy (*Heathers* [1988]). By the 1990s, teen films were an established genre – or, at the very least, a subgenre – with their own recognisable style, conventions and archetypes.

32

THE CRAFT

It is the existence of this store of conventions and archetypes, the cinematic grammar of the teen film, that enabled Andrew Fleming to create a filmic representation of witchcraft that was not defined by what he dismisses as a fantasy cliché of hags in "black pointy hats with green skin" (Jacobs and Brucculieri), but rather by the painful realities of adolescence. Like many teen films before it, *The Craft* portrays high school as a microcosm of wider society, with all of its social prejudices and hierarchies replicated in miniature. Henry Giroux argues that films about youth and representations of adolescence generally function as "signposts that register society's own crises of community, vision, and meaning" (qtd. in Lee 2). When Sarah first enters her new high school, the framing and camerawork suggest that she is also entering a new world. A high crane shot captures Sarah from above as she makes her way through the new school entrance, disappearing into a crowd of seemingly identical teens. Upon entering the school, Sarah is immediately coded as an outsider: she is the only student not wearing a school uniform. Although costume designer Deborah Everton claims that Sarah's visual difference stemmed from a delay in the wardrobe department (Jacobs and Brucculieri), the fact that Sarah has not yet procured a uniform renders her visually distinct from the other students, and she is already marked as different. This empowers her to act as a point-of-view character, an audience avatar, through whose perspective we are introduced to the complex social structures of a typical American high school.

The Craft apes popular high school films of the era by presenting the school environment as its own distinct social system, made up of different character types who each occupy their own unique positions in the social hierarchy: we have the blonde bully Laura Lizzie, the selfish jock Chris, the stoner Mitt (Breckin Meyer) and the innocent new girl Sarah. This representation of high school as a social body comprised of diverse social "types" is very much a feature of eighties and nineties American cinema. In many teen films, the diversity of the high school experience is represented through what Roz Kaveney terms the "anthropology shot", a pan or cut to "stock shots of the various high school cliques to indicate their social division – the alternative crowd, the sorority sisters and fraternity brothers crowd, the nerd crowd, the ethnic crowd" (Lee 2). While *The Craft* incorporates a broad array of social types, it does not utilise this kind of explicit anthropological overview of the school environment. Instead, both the dialogue and the framing of the coven serve to position the girls in opposition to the rest of the student body. Numerous scenes frame the girls at the centre of the camera's gaze as they move in slow motion, ignoring or expressing scorn towards the other students who exist on the periphery of their vision. In other scenes the girls are shot from a distance as other characters, usually rendered in close-ups or medium shots, glance anxiously towards them. Again, this signifies the girls' alienation from their peers.

Additionally, the witches are set off from their peers through their style of dress, which is often dark and gothic. By the mid-nineties, the alternative grunge style that had emerged alongside the music exported from rainy Seattle by bands like Nirvana, Hole, Pearl Jam, Soundgarden and others had become mainstream. The flannel shirts, leather jackets and layers of ill-fitting clothes that defined this style had long since been co-opted by high fashion, with designer Marc Jacobs basing his spring/summer 1993 collection on the grunge look and "heroin chic" models dominating runways (Troy 105). This mainstreaming of grunge appears in *The Craft*, as jock Chris Hooker and his friends sport flannel shirts over their school uniforms. Rochelle, Nancy, Bonnie and Sarah are distinguished from this vaguely grungy, mid-nineties milieu by their dark, gothic style of dress. In an interview with the *Huffington Post*, Fleming claimed that he did not want his teen witches to look like fairy tale monsters or Halloween hags. Instead, he wanted to costume them as though they were members of eighties goth band The Cure. Although the girls attend a Catholic high school and are expected to wear a conservative uniform, they modify their outfits to reflect a gothic aesthetic: they add more items of black clothing, wear stockings and suspenders, shorten their skirts, sport ankhs and repurposed rosary beads as necklaces, and they wear dramatic, dark make-up. In doing so, the girls not only distinguish themselves from their comparatively bland classmates and visually hint at their true, witchy nature, they also subvert the emblems of adult and religious authority by transforming their Catholic uniforms into dark, gothic garb.

Like many high school films, *The Craft* presents the school itself as a stage on which young people can play out their own dramas of social and personal development. The educational purpose of the building is therefore incidental to its function as the site of inter- and intragenerational conflict, the process of self-definition that constitutes "growing up". In his essay, "Teens, Parties, and Rollercoasters: A Genre of the 90s", Robin Wood notes that in school-centric films "sex is the structuring presence, education is the structuring absence" (314). Wood claims that while the teenagers in these films

THE CRAFT

often seem scornful of their teachers and reluctant to study, "education is tolerated but never challenged because to challenge or attack the education system is to challenge or attack capitalism" (315). *The Craft* replicates this vision of the school as a social rather than an educational space. The lessons the girls learn in the classroom are simply a backdrop to the discovery of their witchy powers and their attempts to navigate nascent adult identities. Wood also notes that in the typical teen film not only is the principal function of the school – education – relegated to background noise over which the dramas of adolescence can play out, but the protagonists' home lives are also generally ill-defined (319). In *The Craft*, we are provided with glimpses into each coven member's family life – with the notable exception of Rochelle, which will be discussed in Chapter 3. Yet, while the girls are undeniably influenced by their familial situations – Sarah's relationship with her dead mother even proves pivotal in her victory over Nancy – their lives centre primarily around peer interaction and their intense friendships with each other. In this way, it seems that *The Craft* is structured around the same concerns that define the standard nineties high school film: the protagonists are largely disconnected from education and family, their focus instead turned towards sex, relationships and the process of becoming an individual.

Much of the popularity accrued by *The Craft* is largely due to the innovative way in which it draws, often rather explicitly, on the conventions of contemporary teen films. As Emily Chandler notes in her article "'Loving and Cruel, All at the Same Time': Girlhood Identity in *The Craft*", this is a film that not only reflects, but actively "constitutes girls' identities by subverting teen film tropes within discourses of gender and girlhood, such as popularity, friendship, and aggression" (111). The school environment at the heart of the film is the centre of the teenage universe, and it is a space of growth, self-development, cruelty and unity. *The Craft* fuses the grammar of popular jocks, classroom taunts and intense friendships with the fantastic iconography of magical chants, midnight incantations and levitation spells. In his analysis of nineties horror cinema, Muir observes that the young women in *The Craft* do not use witchcraft to conjure up demons, fly on broomsticks or transform themselves into wondrous creatures. Instead, the girls use their supernatural powers to seduce boys and seek revenge on the bullies who cruelly abuse them (40). Somewhat dismissively, he notes that *The Craft* does not depart in any kind of radical manner from the generic conventions of the standard teen film: "The rules of high school thus remain the same, only the clique at the top of the food chain has changed" (40). However, it is this fixity of high school norms that makes *The Craft* so unique and enduring. Its witches are not fantasy creatures, monstrous hags or even participants in an immense Satanic conspiracy (such as the one seen in *Rosemary's Baby* [1968]); they are simply ordinary teenage girls, young women who express the same hopes and desires as adolescents the world over: acceptance, popularity, beauty, love.

Timothy Shary questions the extent to which *The Craft* can be read as a film about the occult, suggesting that "*The Craft* is as much a critique of the perfidy of school cliques as it is of witchcraft" (177). For Shary, as for many fans of the film, *The Craft* is unique because of the way in which it takes the ordinary experiences of adolescence and explicates them through the metamorphic language of the supernatural. The coven, as an intense, exaggerated manifestation of the powerful friendships that often form between young women, embodies the myriad ways in which such relationships can confer support and strength, while also possessing untold potential for destruction and painful dissolution. Throughout *The Craft*, magic serves as a metaphor for the complex transformations of adolescence: when Sarah casts a love spell over football player Chris, he abruptly develops romantic feelings for her. Yet, by virtue of his feelings being manipulated through magic, his love quickly becomes dark, twisted and obsessive. Ultimately, he attempts to rape Sarah when she runs away from his fumbled embraces in a parked car. This relationship and its turn towards violence reflects the manner in which adolescent romance can quickly escalate in intensity and transform into something altogether more disturbing. While this metaphor is, as noted previously, problematic due to the implication that Sarah is responsible for his assault, the film's use of the fantastic to express the difficulties inherent in growing up facilitates a new perspective on the adolescent experience.

SLASHER ELEMENTS IN *THE CRAFT*

While *The Craft* draws extensively on conventions associated with teen comedies, dramas and romances, it also borrows heavily from another perennial teen favourite, the slasher. A ubiquitous feature of the teenage movie-going experience, slashers account for nearly one-third of all teen horror films produced since 1980 and have

THE CRAFT

consistently earned more at the box office than any other incarnation of teen horror (Shary 148). Although the slasher, with its punitive attitude towards sexuality, had begun to fall out of favour as the conservative consensus of the 1980s gave way to the more divisive nineties, the genre was reinvigorated in the middle of the decade when Wes Craven released his immensely successful *Scream* (1996) (164). For its time, *Scream* was a unique addition to the slasher canon. First, in contrast to many of the popular incarnations of the subgenre that appeared in the 1970s and 1980s, its masked killers are neither adults nor outsiders; they are teenagers themselves, members of the core group of youths stalked by the initially anonymous murderer (West 9). Consequently, while films like *Halloween* might depict "the night he came home" – the return of an exiled monster to the community that banished him – in nineties teen slashers the horror was always at home (9). The killers that stalked teenagers in the final decade of the twentieth century were less likely to be escaped lunatics or legendary monsters, and more likely to be friends, lovers or family members. As noted at the beginning of this chapter, the nineties was a period during which America's national anxieties began to turn inward. The collapse of the Soviet Union and the disintegration of the Eastern European communist bloc robbed the United States of its longstanding international adversary. At the same time, a series of violent occurrences, from the brutal beating of Rodney King to the Oklahoma City bombing, led many Americans to look within their own borders – as well as within their own homes and communities – for enemies.

The Craft, which was released in the same year as *Scream* – pre-dating the iconic meta-slasher by only a few months – replicates this pattern of intragenerational violence. The film undoubtedly presents us with violent or threatening adults, such as Nancy's stepfather and the homeless snake-handler; however, the most spectacular acts of violence that occur in the film take place amongst the teenagers. High school, it seems, is a dangerous and predatory space. On Sarah's first day at Benedict's Academy, we see numerous shots of security guards patrolling the campus, a reminder that the 1990s was a decade which saw a marked increase in school shootings. Sexual harassment also appears rampant on campus. Even before Chris attempts to rape Sarah, we see numerous examples of bullying related to a perceived lack or abundance of female sexuality. Chris spreads cruel rumours about Nancy's "promiscuity", while later his friends join in as he torments Sarah after she refuses to sleep with him. As the film progresses, we see the witches take sadistic revenge on their peers: Rochelle causes racist bully Laura Lizzie to lose her hair in a painful and traumatic manner, and during one of the film's most disturbing scenes, Nancy uses her powers to propel an intoxicated Chris through a window to his death. In the film's climax, Nancy comes to Sarah's house with the intention of punishing her for betraying the coven. After convincing Sarah that her parents have been killed, Nancy slits Sarah's wrists and screams that Sarah should just die since she has already destroyed those around her. When she attempts to flee, Rochelle, Nancy and Bonnie conjure up visions of rats, snakes and maggots, which rain down on Sarah. The violence in these scenes is brutal and intense, but what makes it even more disturbing is that the girls who abuse Sarah so cruelly were once her closest friends, her sister witches.

In her book on gender and psychology, Linda Brannon describes two types of popular film that portray violence against women. The first of these is the "slasher", while the second is what she terms "mean girl movies", films in which cattiness and competition between women ultimately escalate to outright violence (196). Brannon argues that these "mean girl movies" (which include *Foxfire* (1996), *Jawbreaker* (1999) and, of course, *The Craft*) feature women who are abused by men *and* tormented by other women – and consequently they often contain more violence against women than slashers (196). *The Craft*, however, can be differentiated from the standard "mean girl movie" by its use of horror tropes and the manner in which its climax adheres to a number of the key conventions of the slasher film. In particular, the final confrontation between Sarah and Nancy takes on the guise of a conventional slasher chase wherein the killer pursues a young woman through a dark, empty house. The rage-filled Nancy is abandoned by Rochelle and Bonnie after they glimpse a vision of the consequences that could stem from their improper use of magic. Alone, she pursues Sarah through her home, clad in a long black dress and wielding a knife. Although *The Craft* deals rather explicitly with the realm of the supernatural, the ultimate confrontation between Sarah and Nancy draws explicitly (and, indeed, rather self-consciously) on the visual lexicon of the slasher genre.

Perhaps the most overt trope that *The Craft* borrows from the slasher film is the figure of the "final girl". An enduring feature of the slasher, the concept of the final girl owes its origin to Carol J. Clover's iconic study, *Men, Women and Chain Saws: Gender in the Modern Horror Film* (1992). In this book, Clover defines the final girl as the survivor: "the one who encounters the mutilated bodies of her friends and perceives the full extent of the preceding horror and of her own peril; who is chased, cornered, wounded; whom we see scream, stagger, fall, rise, and scream again" (35). The final girl is a key component of the slasher genre, the victimised girl who alone defeats, or at least escapes from, the killer. She is usually level-headed, sensible and innocent in comparison to her often-promiscuous friends. She is traditionally the only character to be developed in any psychological detail (44), and she is typically androgynous, usually bearing a name of indeterminate gender like Laurie (*Halloween*), Stretch (*Texas Chain Saw Massacre Part 2*) or Sidney (*Scream*). As Clover notes, "The gender of the Final Girl is likewise compromised from the outset by her masculine interests, her inevitable sexual reluctance, her apartness from other girls, sometimes her name" (48). Although Sarah appears traditionally feminine, with her definitively female name and often girlish dress sense, she does fit many of the final girl criteria. She is more sensible, reserved and mature than her fellow witches. She is apprehensive and cautious about magic, and when she does use it, she understands that there are limitations and rules that must be adhered to. She is less sexually aggressive than Nancy and, later, Bonnie. She is initially reluctant to join the coven, and she doesn't shoplift. Sarah occupies the role of the good girl and, consequently, she uses her virtue, practicality and good sense to survive her attack by the coven. While she may be tempted by the promise of infinite power, she does not succumb to its allure, and so she retains the strength of character necessary to survive. Her final strike against Nancy, the blow that ultimately defeats her, comes when Sarah cleverly vanishes into the floor against which she has been pinned, leaving behind only her empty clothes. When the crazed Nancy leans in to inspect the spot where Sarah should be lying, raising her knife above her head, Sarah quickly rematerialises and kicks Nancy with supernatural force.

Although it cannot be claimed that *The Craft* is simply a slasher with witches – this would be a far too simplistic analysis of a complex and multifaceted film – it does draw on the conventions of the slasher film, particularly in its characterisation of Sarah as the responsible, level-headed girl who uses her talents and moral sense to survive the horror that besieges her. Moreover, *The Craft* plays with the gender dynamics of the standard Hollywood slasher; rather than portraying an innocent young woman stalked by a masked man, Fleming's film instead depicts a conflict between women. Although some have seen this as a problematic re-inscription of the age-old trope of the "catty" woman, *The Craft* uses this conflict as an analogue for the process of growing up, becoming an individual and learning to negotiate difficult interpersonal relationships. The reimagining of the archetypal chase between the final girl and killer as a magically inflected fight between Sarah and Nancy embodies these notions of growth and articulates the value of freeing oneself from toxic relationships, whether romantic or platonic.

Although, *The Craft* is undeniably a supernatural horror film – a contemporary tale of witchcraft and wonder – it is also a product of nineties Hollywood, and, as such, it could not fail to be influenced by the cinematic context from which it emerged. One such source of inspiration was clearly the teen slasher with its knife-wielding "psychos" and valiant final girls; another source was the teen comedy or romance – the standard cinematic coming-of-age tale – with its store of recognisable cliques and high school drama. *The Craft* is, in many ways, a cinematic hybrid that brings together components of various popular cinematic genres aimed at teenagers. It is a high school film, a horror film, a story of growing up, and it even possesses elements of the slasher. Yet, rather than being derivative, *The Craft* is dynamic, enduring largely due to its capacity to synthesise diverse cinematic conventions. Even more so, it remains a landmark on the map of late twentieth-century horror cinema, largely due to this generic hybridity.

Chapter 2: "Satanic Panic": A New Witch for the Nineties

Early in *The Craft*, popular jock Chris informs Sarah that the trio of school outcasts – Rochelle, Nancy and Bonnie – are rumoured to be "witches". Chris's description of the girls as witches carries with it a host of cultural connotations, both modern and ancient. His language initially connects witchcraft to socially undesirable categories; Nancy, we are told, is a "slut", while Bonnie has scars covering large sections of her body. Witchcraft, then, is linked to both "ugliness" and promiscuity. However, the girl's status as witches also conjures a wider array of associations, from John Updike's *The Witches of Eastwick* (1984) and the then-recent "Satanic Panic" to early modern witchcraft beliefs. The category of "witch" is thus revealed to be an extraordinarily broad descriptor, and it is this multivalence – this capacity for multiple meanings – that *The Craft* deploys in its representation of witchcraft. Although now considered one of cinema's most influential portrayals of witchcraft, *The Craft* draws heavily on existing representations and mythologies in its postmodern, self-aware exploration of magic, power and desire. Indeed, much of the film's potency lies in its capacity to transform and subvert ingrained ideas about witchcraft.

This chapter positions *The Craft* within the broader history of witchcraft lore, exploring not only how the film incorporates popular cultural representations of witches but also how it draws on historical beliefs and archetypes. The witches in *The Craft* are amalgamations of more than five centuries' worth of shifting conceptions of witchcraft and its practitioners. Consequently, the viewer's experience of the film becomes infinitely richer when the film is viewed in the context of this history. The pages that follow aim to provide some sense of the complex, often contradictory, cultural discourses that shaped *The Craft*'s adolescent witches by outlining a brief history of witchcraft in the Western imagination, the role of the witch in popular entertainment, and the late twentieth-century re-emergence of the witch as a real-world concern following both the creation of Wicca and the Satanic Panic of the 1980s and early 1990s.

DEFINING WITCHCRAFT: WHAT IS A WITCH AND WHERE DOES SHE COME FROM?

In his introduction to the study of witchcraft, the scholar Malcolm Gaskill attempts to articulate the conceptual and historical fluidity of the witch:

> Meanings of witchcraft are so varied because the concept is so versatile. Wicca is a recognized religion whose adherents call themselves "witches". Children's fiction, horror films, and newspaper cartoons all make use of witches, drawing on shared ideas and imagery. "Witch-hunt" commonly describes even modest antagonisms and injustices, and "witch" remains an insult commonly directed at women. (5)

The witch is both modern and ancient. She exists in the mythology of the ancient world, but contemporary practitioners of the Neopagan faith Wicca also describe themselves as witches. The witch appears in the fantastic realm of fairy tale, but she is also a historical reality. She stalks the night terrors of small children, but she also represents a crime for which laws were passed and lives were taken. Discussing witchcraft is therefore a surprisingly difficult task. The word "witch" encompasses so much and evokes different connotations across cultures and eras.

According to witchcraft historian Ronald Hutton, witches can, nevertheless, be identified through a number of shared traits. Witches are generally a direct threat to others, utilising supernatural methods to bring about injury, suffering or misfortune (Hutton, *Witch* 3). Unlike other enemies, witches are internal rather than external threats to the community; they bring suffering to family, friends and neighbours (3). At the same time, witches are rarely isolated figures. They typically work within a tradition, weaving their magic through esoteric rites which can be taught to others or passed down along the generations (3). Witches are anti-social beings, who reject all that is good, holy or right by aligning themselves with malevolent supernatural forces or entering into a pact with the Devil (4). Lastly, witches are not omnipotent. They can be resisted through counter-magic or forced to lift their spells following legal or social pressure (4). Beyond these unifying features, witches are a diverse lot. The standard witch can vary according to age and gender. In some cultures, witches are male, in others they are female, and in still others they can be either. During the European witch trials (c. 1450–1750), approximately 75 per cent to 80 per cent of the 40,000 to 60,000 individuals executed

THE CRAFT

were female (Thurston 147). However, outside of Western Europe, in more remote regions, like Iceland, only 10 per cent of those killed were women (Behringer 39).

In many parts of the world, witches signify notions of perversion, the reversal of all that a given society holds sacred. Witches engage in taboo, socially unacceptable activities, like incest, public nudity and cannibalism (Hutton, *Witch* 22). Often, they meet at night when righteous, law-abiding members of society are asleep: they are active and powerful at the precise moment that everyone else is inactive and vulnerable (22). In some figurations, these notions of inversion are literalised. Hutton observes that the Zulu believed witches travelled by riding backwards on a baboon (*Witch* 23). Likewise, one of the most influential European portrayals of a witch, Albrecht Dürer's *Witch Riding on a Goat* (1500), exemplifies similar notions of reversal and the upending of cultural norms (Figure 6).

Figure 6. Witch Riding on a Goat *by Albrecht Dürer (1500). Image: Public domain via Wikimedia Commons*

43

Belief in witchcraft can be traced all the way back to antiquity. In ancient Greece, unofficial magicians often performed services beyond what priests and religious leaders could provide, arousing suspicion because of a perceived attempt to usurp state power (Gaskill 11). However, despite the antique origins of witchcraft beliefs, the popular vision of the witch – the devil-worshipping sorceress riding a broomstick – is comparatively new, first appearing during the early modern period (c. 1450–1800). This night-flying witch, whose powers stem from a pact with the devil, is often referred to as the "composite" or "cumulative" concept of witchcraft. This stereotype is, according to Brian P. Levack, a composite because of how it synthesised formerly unconnected ideas about magic, while it can be considered cumulative because these ideas built gradually upon or supplanted one another. Emerging only in the early years of the fifteenth century, the composite stereotype of the witch hinged on the notion of Satanic witchcraft: the witch was a "maleficent magician who made a pact with the Devil and worshipped him with other witches at the sabbath" (Levack).

In many European jurisdictions, the legal definition of witchcraft hinged on the notion that a witch was empowered to practise harmful magic by virtue of a pact made with the Devil (Levack). A second and related feature of this Satanic witch was that she engaged in communal worship of the Devil during a meeting called a sabbath (Levack). At these sabbaths, witches were believed to engage in infanticide, cannibalism and sexual intercourse with the Devil or his demons. Lastly, witches were said to possess the power of flight. Sometimes, witches rode animals to their Satanic gatherings, while other artistic representations portrayed them riding rods or sticks (Levack). The most iconic tool of flight, the broomstick, is one that has accrued a wealth of symbolic associations over the centuries. Not only is the broom associated with traditionally feminine domestic chores, but it is also linked to fertility rites, and functions as a phallic symbol (Levack). Transforming a symbol of domestic order into a tool of diabolic magic, the witch is once again seen to upend social norms and pervert community values.

Despite its contemporary setting, *The Craft* repeatedly alludes to traits and practices associated with the Satanic witch, while at the same time gesturing forward to twentieth-century reinventions of witchcraft. As a product of the thoroughly self-aware, playfully postmodern 1990s, *The Craft* frequently conjures up historical ideas about witchcraft only to dismiss them as outmoded or archaic. One of the first such attempts

THE CRAFT

to banish ingrained notions about witchery is an explicit rejection of the Devil as the traditional witch's master. Following Sarah's first trip to the magic store with Rochelle, Nancy and Bonnie, the girls retire to a park where they lounge on abandoned furniture and discuss the future of their coven. Sarah's immediate assumption is that her new friends worship the Devil, a stereotype they are quick to dismiss. The coven laughs at Sarah, and Nancy explains that the being they invoke in their rites goes beyond human constructs like God and the Devil. The deity they appeal to is Manon, a fabrication for the purposes of the film, whom they describe as encompassing *everything*. Manon is the air, the trees, the sky and the earth. In one of the film's most famous lines of dialogue, Nancy tells Sarah that "if God and the Devil were playing football, Manon would be the stadium that they played on. It would be the sun that shone down on them". A symbol of the natural world, Manon is remote from binary conceptions of good and evil.

The Craft also addresses the other key features of the composite/cumulative concept of the Satanic witch: the sabbath and nocturnal flight. However, the manner in which *The Craft* reimagines both flight and the sabbath underscores two of the film's key themes: the complexity of adolescence and the alternately powerful and destructive nature of female friendship. The film reimagines the witches' sabbath, or meeting, in the context of New Age spirituality and Wicca (see below). Rather than a horrifying spectacle of perversion and transgression, the "sabbaths" that appear in the film initially stress and then complicate notions of sisterhood, bonding, and affinity with nature. The first such meeting entails a field trip during which the girls take a bus ride to the remote Wood Ranch in Simi Valley. Set to a contemporary cover of Marianne Faithfull's "Witches' Song", the sequence reinforces the notion that the girls are outsiders with only one another to rely on. While their ultimate purpose is the working of magic, the scene explicitly links witchcraft to female bonding and sisterhood. The ritual they engage in requires each witch to prick her finger and mix a drop of their blood with a cup of wine. As the girls sip the wine, they utter an incantation that begins with the words, "I drink of my sisters". When the ritual is completed, the girls are enveloped in a cloud of butterflies. Rendered through CGI technology, the butterflies indicate that Manon has heard their pleas. Yet, it also suggests a oneness with nature and a solidification of their shared bond.

The second "sabbath" is more unsettling. The girls abscond to a remote beach where they will "Invoke the Spirit". During this meeting, notions of sisterly unity are undermined and the girls' relationship to nature becomes increasingly troubled. A dark mirror of the first ritual, the meeting takes place at night rather than bathed in the golden sunshine that characterised their first sabbath. Unity and sisterly affection are replaced by paranoia and selfishness: where the other girls cry out to the guardians of the four corners to "hear *us*", power-hungry Nancy implores them to "hear *me*". The camerawork reflects this sinister shift in tone, as the camera circles in 360-degree pans (Greene 165), its speed indicating a loss of control and impending chaos. Likewise, where the first such meeting concluded with the girls experiencing a sense of oneness with nature as they are surrounded by gentle, fluttering butterflies, the second meeting suggests fracture and disharmony. The girls awaken the next morning to find dozens of sharks lying dead on the beach. They have severed their connection with the natural world and their desire for power has fractured their sisterly connection.

In a similar manner, the notion of the witches' flight is also modernised and redeployed to comment on the complexity of female friendships. Although the film's teen witches never ride broomsticks through the air, they do practise levitation in what could be seen as a more grounded manifestation of the nocturnal flight. Their first experience of levitation comes in the midst of that most stereotypically feminine of rites, the slumber party. Sarah suggests they play an old party game called "light as a feather, stiff as a board". Sitting in a circle and placing their fingers underneath Rochelle, they lift her off the ground before removing their fingers and leaving Rochelle to float, unsupported, in mid-air. When Bonnie's mother appears at the door with clean towels, the spell is broken and Rochelle crashes to the floor. Bonnie's mother asks if the girls are "getting high in there", and the witches collapse in fits of giggles. Here, the levitation game embodies themes of sisterhood, female friendship and bonding. However, as with the sabbath, when levitation appears again in the film, it is a dark reflection of the rapturous slumber party sequence. The next significant scene involving levitation comes at the end of the film, when Rochelle, Nancy and Bonnie have convinced Sarah that her parents have died in plane crash. In a disturbing parallel to the more common experience of high school bullying, Sarah's former friends attempt to coax her into suicide, as they float, menacingly, in the air above her. Once again, *The Craft* deploys a key facet of historical witchcraft lore to illustrate both the establishment and dissolution of adolescent friendship.

"ARE YOU A GOOD WITCH OR A BAD WITCH?": WITCHES IN POPULAR CULTURE

Although *The Craft* draws extensively on historical ideas about witchcraft, it is also heavily indebted to popular cultural representations of witches. Indeed, the film is overtly self-conscious and often wry about its cinematic and televisual lineage. Chris refers to Rochelle, Nancy and Bonnie as "the Bitches of Eastwick" (a nod to John Updike's 1984 novel *The Witches of Eastwick* and its 1987 cinematic adaptation), and the girls watch the supernatural sitcom *Bewitched* at a slumber party (Figure 7). *The Craft* clearly situates itself within a lengthy tradition of pop cultural witches, at once echoing and subverting ingrained ideas about witchcraft.

Figure 7. The girls watch the popular 1960s sitcom Bewitched. *Image: Photofest*

Witches have always had a place in mass culture. Even before the emergence of modern popular media – cinema, television, paperback novels – the witch was a ubiquitous presence in oral culture. In myths and folktales, witches haunt the wild spaces of woodlands and mountain peaks. They are sorceresses who transform men into swine; wicked hags who fatten and devour small children. Miglena Sternadori notes that the witch – along with sirens, chimeras and other grotesque beings – reflects the "female monster" archetype in her capacity to embody male anxieties about womanhood (303). At the same time, although the witch may be popularly assumed to serve as the apotheosis of male anxieties about femininity, there is also a degree to which she echoes women's anxieties about their identities, homes and families. Diane Purkiss argues that while historians have popularly framed the witch as the church's Other – the dark opposite of masculine religious power – it is also possible to understand the witch as woman's Other, her shadowy alter ego (102). After all, if woman, as wife and mother, is primarily tasked with maintaining order and cleanliness in the home, providing her family with nutritious meals and nurturing devotion, the witch, with her arsenal of poisons and curses, represents an inversion of the good wife. In stories such as "Snow White" or "Hansel and Gretel" the witch who offers food to the protagonists – a poisoned apple, luxuriant gingerbread – usurps the role of the good mother, "since it was normally a maternal duty to offer food and guard its integrity" (Purkiss 289). Purkiss observes that traditionally the housewife's role was defined by the need to maintain the boundaries that safeguarded the family home: "boundaries between nature and culture, between inside and outside, pollution and purity" (103). The witch, however, violates these boundaries; she poisons food that should be healthful, leaves fetishes near thresholds and brings evil to the happy home.

During the early modern period, witches were a central component of the popular imagination. They played a key role in entertainment, appearing regularly in literature, theatre and the visual arts. In 1584, an MP and engineer from Kent named Reginald Scot published the first extant treatise on witchcraft by an English author (Davies 381). Scot was sceptical about the existence of witchcraft and claimed that the phenomenon was "incomprehensible to the wise, learned or faithfull; a probable matter to children, fooles, melancholike persons and papists" (382). His treatise, *The Discouerie of Witchcraft*, argued that belief in witchcraft was facilitated by ignorance. Witchcraft was, for Scot, a relic of Catholic superstitions that had survived the Reformation and promulgated faith in blessed objects, relics, saints and spirits (382). Although *The Discouerie of Witchcraft*

THE CRAFT

was condemned by many writers on the subject, including King James I, the work nevertheless inspired numerous authors, playwrights and poets. Witchcraft historian Marion Gibson observes that Scot's work had "an important afterlife in texts like Shakespeare's *Macbeth*, Jonson's *The Masque of Queenes* and Middleton's *The Witch*" (*Basics* 64). Gibson argues that Scot's discourse on witchcraft as an imagined threat rather than a real crime helped to transform the witch from a source of political and cultural anxiety into a literary symbol. It is for this reason that most plays and poems produced between the 1590s and 1630s portray their witches as entertaining figures, more metaphorical than realistic (*Basics* 67). Furthermore, the plethora of stories that Scot collected in his attempts to disprove witchcraft superstitions frequently made their way into contemporary works of fiction. Demonic entities drawn from Scot's *Discouerie*, as well as anecdotes about the disruptive antics of witches and spirits, reappeared in William Shakespeare's *A Midsummer Night's Dream* (1595/6) and *Macbeth* (1606).

By the nineteenth century, this construction of the witch as a symbol was deeply ingrained in both political rhetoric and popular culture. In 1863, the French historian Jules Michelet published *La sorcière* (usually translated as *Satanism and Witchcraft*), a study of medieval and early modern occultism that framed witchcraft as a revolt on the part of European peasants against the stranglehold of the aristocracy and the Catholic Church. For Michelet, witchcraft and folk magic were acts of rebellion against ingrained power structures, their subversive spirit anticipating that of the French Revolution. Three decades later, the American suffragist Matilda Joslyn Gage identified the witch hunts of previous centuries as evidence of "women's age-old oppression by men" (Gibson, *American* 113). In her 1893 book, *Woman, Church and State*, Gage claimed that the nineteenth-century subjugation of women was akin to the early-modern witch trials, arguing that women were persecuted for witchcraft because their wisdom constituted an inherent threat to the power wielded by the church (Grossman, *Waking* 23). Later, in her seminal feminist essay "A Room of One's Own" (1929), Virginia Woolf maintained that women accused of witchcraft in the past were really creative individuals, poets and novelists, persecuted by a society that didn't understand them. By the middle decades of the twentieth century, the notion that the witch could simultaneously represent both female oppression and empowerment had gained sufficient cultural cachet that a feminist activist group could appropriate both the iconography and the language of witchcraft for their protests. Naming themselves W.I.T.C.H. (Women's International Terrorist Conspiracy from Hell), the group was founded in the late 1960s and would publicly hex political figures who opposed the push for women's rights.

Nineteenth-century writers such as Michelet and Gage not only helped to establish the witch as a feminist icon, they also helped to popularise the concept of "good witches" by figuring those targeted by witch hunts as oppressed forerunners of contemporary social activists and political revolutionaries. Gage, however, went even further, by inspiring one of the most enduring figurations of the good witch: "Glinda the Good". L. Frank Baum, author of *The Wonderful Wizard of Oz* (1900), was Gage's son-in-law, and her descriptions of wise and powerful women, oppressed by male-dominated institutions, appear to have influenced Baum's own benevolent sorceresses. Moreover, as Marion Gibson observes, Baum's witches inaugurated a new, "antihistorical" conception of the witch, freed from "references to records, histories, or demonologies" (*American* 140). Witchcraft was untethered from its historical associations with the Satanic witch and the violence of the witch trials. Now, the witch could be imagined in new and increasingly creative ways.

It may be as a result of this new creativity, unleashed around the turn of the twentieth century, that witches appeared regularly in early cinema. In "trick films" – short silent films created to demonstrate new special effects – witches were popular figures. Their enchantments and magical spells served as the ideal pretext for the transformations and disappearances that abound in early films such as *The Enchanted Well* (1903) and *The Witch* (1906), both directed by French filmmaker and illusionist Georges Méliès. In 1908, the first recorded American film to make use of the witch archetype was released by Vitagraph. Also entitled *The Witch*, this film was less of a trick film and more of a historical picture set during the European witch hunts of the early modern period (Greene 19). Similarly, Swedish director Benjamin Christensen's *Häxan*, or *Witchcraft Through the Ages* (1921), became one of the first films to approach witchcraft as a serious, historical subject (Russell 116). Yet, despite the ubiquity of witches in early cinema, it was not until the release of MGM's adaptation of Baum's *Wonderful Wizard of Oz* that the witch became fixed in the American imagination. Indeed, *The Wizard of Oz*'s villainous Wicked Witch has probably done more to shape popular perceptions of the witch than any other figure, fictional or historical (de Blécourt 257).

The Wicked Witch of the West, as she appears in the 1939 musical, has little in common with previous iterations of the character. Significantly, Baum's original Wicked Witch did not have green skin (Greene 59). Illustrations, paintings and earlier adaptations also made no mention of her greenish pallor (59). Rather, the Wicked Witch's green make-up arose as a result of the Technicolor process used in the film. Margaret Hamilton, the actress who played the iconic villain, described how black clothing, when placed directly next to the skin and filmed in three-strip Technicolor, results in an optical illusion that makes it appear as though the actor's limbs and head are disconnected from their black-clad body (59). By covering Hamilton in green make-up, the MGM costume designers not only solved the visual problem created by early Technicolor film, but they also crafted the popular image of the green-skinned witch that would endure for decades to come.

Figure 8. Good vs bad witches in The Wizard of Oz (1939). Image: Photofest

At the same time, The Wizard of Oz was responsible for establishing an imaginative binary that divided witchcraft into polarised positions of good versus evil. The Wizard of Oz drew on, and ultimately solidified, a motif already common in fairy tales, whereby goodness is equated with beauty, and evil with ugliness. Despite the folkloric lineage of this trope, the binary opposition between the ugly, cruel Wicked Witch of the West and the beautiful, angelic Glinda the Good proved especially influential, shaping popular images of good and bad witches as both morally and aesthetically dichotomous. In a recent (2019) article for *The Atlantic*, author and practising witch Pam Grossman used the occasion of *The Wizard of Oz*'s 80th anniversary to muse on the film's conflation of "prettiness and virtue". In particular, Grossman dwells on Glinda's famous assertion that "Only bad witches are ugly", and while the line between good (beautiful) and bad (ugly) witches may have wavered and become increasingly permeable in subsequent decades, Glinda's aphorism remains a potent one (Figure 8).

Magic shop owner Lirio may be quick to tell Sarah that "True magic is neither black, nor white", but *The Craft* is nevertheless swift to separate the good witches from the bad. Sarah, who is a natural witch and initially reluctant to explore the occult, is juxtaposed with her more-selfish, rebellious cohorts early in the film. Notably, Sarah listens carefully to Lirio's words of wisdom while her new friends snicker contemptuously. Later, Sarah is the only one to express concern about the nature of the coven's practices. Much like *The Wizard of Oz*, the binary *The Craft* establishes between good and bad witches also relies on problematic notions about morality and "proper" femininity. It is significant, and somewhat unsettling, that Sarah is framed not only as more virtuous than her peers, but that her goodness is connected to her status as a white, able-bodied, upper-middle-class woman. Sarah's witchcraft is inherent, passed down from an idealised mother who died in childbirth. Her magic is presented as natural and pure. Conversely, the marginal social positions occupied by working-class Nancy, African American Rochelle and disfigured Bonnie mark them out as "bad witches". In contrast to Sarah, they are not natural witches, but interlopers who have co-opted the Craft for selfish and vengeful purposes. In *The Craft*, as in *The Wizard of Oz*, there are good witches and bad. Moreover, in LA, as in Oz, good witches are associated with whiteness, purity and beauty, while the ranks of the bad witches are occupied by those who do not adhere to mainstream, Eurocentric notions of beauty.

Drawing from a range of popular cultural artefacts, *The Craft* is in many ways a bricolage of different constructions of witchcraft. Although bearing traces of a diverse array of literary and cinematic influences, one of the central sources informing the film is the mid-twentieth-century "domestic" witch. In a number of films released during and after the Second World War, witches are portrayed as ordinary women. Still equipped with magical powers and the ability to upend social norms, witches of this period are glamorous, fashionable young women. Their appearance does not single them out as witches, and they inhabit our mundane reality rather than a distant realm of fantasy. Often, these modern witches utilise their magic powers – if they indeed manage to retain them after marriage – in a familial or domestic context, suggesting that feminine power is acceptable so long as it is contained within the home and employed for appropriately feminine ends. Released in 1942, René Clair's comedy *I Married a Witch* stars Veronica Lake as Jennifer, a seventeenth-century Salem witch who reappears in the twentieth century to punish a descendant of those responsible for her execution (Figure 9). In classic screwball comedy style, Jennifer and her intended victim (Frederic March) fall in love. At the end of the film, Jennifer renounces her magical powers and gives up witchcraft to marry and start a family.

Figure 9. Domestic witch Jennifer (Veronica Lake) in I Married a Witch *(1942). Image: Photofest*

Almost two decades later, Richard Quine's *Bell, Book and Candle* (1958) similarly integrates its witches into contemporary American society. Echoing themes and narrative devices found in *I Married a Witch*, *Bell, Book and Candle* portrays its witches as urbane and modern. The film's protagonist is a witch named Gillian (Kim Novak).

Free-spirited and intellectual, Gillian has a degree in anthropology and runs a gallery dedicated to African art. She lives in Greenwich Village – then a hub for members of the Beat Generation and the burgeoning counterculture – with her brother Nicky (Jack Lemmon) and her eccentric aunt Queenie (Elsa Lanchester). Again, the young, beautiful witch falls in love with a human man (here played by Jimmy Stewart) and exchanges her magic for conventional domesticity (Figure 10). Although Gillian's transformation from sultry bohemian to floral-skirted wife in waiting is often a source of disappointment for modern viewers, her desire to embrace middle-American normalcy is very much in keeping with post-war attitudes toward home and family – institutions that were consistently valorised following the trauma of war. Most importantly, however, *Bell, Book and Candle*, like *I Married a Witch*, helped to solidify a contemporary vision of the witch as simply a woman. Neither historical tragedies nor fantastic creatures, Gillian and Jennifer show that witches can be ordinary women or girls who happen to possess great power.

Figure 10. Modern witch Gillian (Kim Novak) with the object of her affection Shep (Jimmy Stewart) and her "familiar" Pyewacket. Image: Photofest

This vision of the witch as a fashionable modern woman also carried over from film to television, influencing one of the twentieth century's most iconic fictional witches: Samantha Stevens. The star of long-running sitcom *Bewitched* (1964–1972), Samantha

(Elizabeth Montgomery) is in many ways an average mid-century American woman. In the first episode of the series, Samantha marries Darrin Stevens (Dick York; later Dick Sargent), an advertising executive with fairly conventional aspirations. After confessing that she is a witch, Samantha promises that she will renounce the occult and live as an ordinary suburban housewife. Most of the show's 254 episodes centre around Darrin's attempts at upward social mobility (securing prestigious advertising accounts; inviting his boss over for dinner) being thwarted either by Samantha's magic going awry or through the interference of her overbearing mother Endora (Agnes Moorehead). In *Bewitched*, the occult is presented primarily as a comedic inconvenience, one which alternately ridicules and bolsters the era's domestic ideology. Despite the chaos they engender, witches are nevertheless presented as superficially normal women, capable of blending in with their wider social milieu while also wielding exceptional magical abilities. That being said, the power wielded by the witch wife is always limited, controlled and carefully circumscribed by the boundaries of domesticity.

This notion of ostensibly normal witches undoubtedly influenced *The Craft* and certainly contributed to its enduring popularity. The four witches at the centre of the film appear to be average teenage girls. Andrew Fleming claimed that he cast Rachel True as Rochelle because she reminded him of a girl he knew in high school. In an interview with the *Huffington Post*, he also suggested that the characters in the film and the choice of actors cast to play them were similarly influenced by his own high school experiences. Describing the character types who would populate *The Craft*, Fleming stated that "Those are the kinds of kids I went to school with, so I thought it would be interesting to see that [in the film]" (Jacobs and Brucculieri). In a similar vein, the characters' costumes, although heavily inflected by the goth subculture and its attendant fashion, are in keeping with the popular trends of the mid-1990s (Jacobs and Brucculieri). Sarah, Rochelle, Nancy and Bonnie are, like Gillian, Jennifer and Samantha, ostensibly ordinary young women. Yet, their apparent mundanity conceals a wealth of magical skill. While the scene in which the four girls laugh, somewhat derisively, at an episode of *Bewitched* can be viewed as a sign of the film's postmodern cynicism, there is also a palpable connection between these works. The mid-century domestic witch, the mundane housewife or average city girl with supernatural abilities, was a cultural archetype that paved the way for films like *The Craft* by unmooring witches from their

DEVIL'S ADVOCATES

associations the distant past and the realms of fantasy. Moreover, just as the magical abilities of the mid-century witch are only acceptable within a domestic setting, so do the occult ambitions of Nancy, Rochelle and Bonnie become increasingly dangerous once they expand beyond small acts of adolescent mischief.

SATANIC PANIC: TEEN WITCHES AND SUBURBAN SATANISTS

The Craft was not, of course, the first text to feature teenage witches. Associations between adolescent girls and the occult extend all the way back to the ascetic saints of the Middle Ages and the spiritualist mediums of the nineteenth century.[1] More recently, historical studies like Marion L. Starkey's *The Devil in Massachusetts* (1949) have framed the accusing circle at the centre of the Salem witch trials as deluded, hysterical teen girls, a view that was taken up by subsequent literary works such as Arthur Miller's play *The Crucible* (1953). In later decades, anxieties about the burgeoning American counterculture resulted in the production of numerous popular films in which young people, and young women in particular, find themselves drawn into Satanic cults. In low-budget films, like *Satan's School for Girls* (1973), the rebellious spirit of the period is conflated with Satanism and witchcraft. The latter part of the 1970s witnessed a multitude of teen-witch films that intentionally played off the success of Brian DePalma's *Carrie* (1976), with an eclectic array of made-for-television movies like *The Spell* (1977), *Stranger in Our House* (1978) and *The Initiation of Sarah* (1978) transposing anxieties about teen rebellion onto tales of witchcraft and cultic rites. By the 1980s, the connection between young people and the occult had adopted an even more sinister guise, as fantasies about clandestine devil-worship proliferated in the media. Consequently, although the 1980s did produce light-hearted representations of adolescent witchcraft, like the comedy *Teen Witch* (1989), the final decades of the twentieth century were defined by a series of paranoid anxieties centred around the supposed connection between young people and the occult.

To consider *The Craft* as a film about witchcraft, it is also important to understand it as a product of the so-called Satanic Panic, and the related "Satanic Ritual Abuse" (SRA) scare, that emerged in the 1980s and continued to generate elaborate visions of murderous witch cults well into the early 1990s. In an interview with the *Huffington*

56

THE CRAFT

Post, screenwriter Peter Filardi claimed that, at the time he and producer Douglas Wick were developing the basic premise of *The Craft*, "I was immersed in the world of teen Satanism and that volatile cocktail of hallucinogens, metal and magic" (Jacobs and Brucculieri). Later, Filardi would go on to write and direct a film called *Ricky 6* (2000) about Ricky Kasso, an American teenager who was accused of killing his friend as part of a Satanically motivated murder in 1984. While *The Craft* does not engage with the paranoid conspiracies that emerged from the Satanic Panic – aside from Sarah's joke that the curtained backroom in Lirio's magic shop might hide "the missing kids from the neighbourhood" – it is necessarily informed by its aftermath and the manner in which the panic deformed popular perceptions of witchcraft.

In her discussion of the Satanic Panic and its relationship with popular culture, Kier-La Janisse notes how the "occult revival" of the late 1960s and 1970s not only saw thousands of young people exploring alternative spiritualities such as neopaganism, Satanism and witchcraft (13), but it also resulted in the consolidation of a reactionary mindset that engendered widespread fears that "there could be occultists living next door" (15). Anton LaVey's establishment of the Church of Satan in 1966 fired the popular imagination, and the Devil swiftly became a ubiquitous presence in film, music and literature. The following year saw the publication of Ira Levin's novel *Rosemary's Baby*, which would be adapted into one of the twentieth century's most influential cinematic representations of Satanic witchcraft. Indeed, the mainstream fascination with the occult was such that *Time* magazine featured two cover stories on the occult revival between 1969 and 1972, with LaVey himself appearing on the cover of *Look* magazine in 1971 (Janisse 13). Moreover, not only did Satan feature prominently in seventies films like *The Exorcist* (1973) and *The Omen* (1976), but his perceived acolytes, Satanists, were cast as villains in works such as *Devil's Rain* and *Race with the Devil* (both 1975) (Janisse 15). It is hardly surprising that by the early 1980s many ordinary Americans believed in the "existence of a vast, underground network of evil Satanic cults sacrificing and abusing children" (Lewis, "Ritual Abuse").

For many historians, the urtext of the Satanic Panic is *Michelle Remembers* (1980), a controversial memoir written by Canadian woman Michelle Smith and her therapist (and eventual husband) Dr Lawrence Padzer. The memoir purports to depict recovered childhood memories of Michelle's abuse at the hands of a Satanic cult. Under hypnosis,

57

DEVIL'S ADVOCATES

Michelle claimed to recall horrendous physical, psychological and sexual abuse carried out against her by the cult, dredging up memories of murder, cannibalism and infanticide (Heller-Nicholas 19). Michelle also maintained that she was dedicated to "His Satanic Majesty" from the age of five (Lewis, "Ritual Abuse"). Given its sensational content, it is unsurprising that *Michelle Remembers* was a cultural phenomenon. Publications such as *People* magazine and the *National Enquirer* presented the book's allegations as fact and catapulted Smith into the media spotlight (Heller-Nicholas 21). Anxieties about Satanism percolated throughout 1980s popular culture. On daytime talk shows like *Oprah* and *Sally Jessie Raphael*, panellists discussed their encounters with the Satanic and "experts" denounced the metastasisation of underground devil worship within the American body politic. In 1988, Geraldo Rivera hosted a two-hour special, *Devil Worship: Exposing Satan's Underground*, during which he interviewed celebrities, victims of alleged SRA, and members of the real-world Church of Satan. The 1980s also witnessed one of the most intensive and lengthy legal prosecutions of individuals implicated in SRA: the McMartin preschool trial. The trial developed out of accusations that a family-run school in Manhattan Beach, California, was a hotbed of Satanic abuse. After a gruelling and sensational trial, the charges against the McMartin preschool staff were eventually dropped, and the defendants were acquitted in 1990 (Lewis, "Ritual Abuse"). Around the same time, the allegations made by Michelle Smith in her best-selling memoir also began to unravel when investigators were unable to verify her story (Heller-Nicholas 28). The Satanic Panic went into remission by around 1992, and after the mid-nineties belief in SRA declined so sharply that it was largely confined to certain groups of conservative Christians (Lewis, "Ritual Abuse").[2]

Nevertheless, the spectre of the Satanic Panic lingers in the background of *The Craft*, informing both the final film and its production history. In particular, the film evinces a clear desire to move away from the SRA scare of the 1980s and separate its high school witches from the stereotype of the teenage Satanist. The filmmakers famously hired Pat Devin, a Wiccan priestess, as a technical consultant. In an interview with John Brightshadow Yohalem, Devin recalls that as well as being intrigued by the script's treatment of magical ethics, she was also drawn to the film by the conspicuous absence of references to Satan: "There was no mention of Satan, aside from the line about if God and the Devil were playing football, Manon would be the stadium: more Gnostic

THE CRAFT

than Wiccan, but a great line". The desire to distance the film from the shadow of Satanism, as well as reaffirming important differences between Satanic practices and Wicca, reflects a conscious rejection of the myths that had grown up around occult belief systems during the 1980s. The Devil is thus evoked only once in the film, and that is verbally, in order to banish him. When Sarah asks, early in the film, "Do you guys worship the devil?", the other girls laugh at her, and Nancy explains that "It's like God and the Devil. I mean, it's everything. It's the trees, it's the ground, it's the rocks, it's the moon … It's everything". Witchcraft is thus distanced from the violence of the eighties SRA panic and is instead aligned with nature and spirituality.

Interviews with Douglas Wick and Peter Filardi indicate that the pair decided to centre their film on witchcraft, not out of a desire to exploit memories of the still-recent Satanic Panic but rather as a means of exploring broader issues of youth, femininity and empowerment. In an oral history published by *Entertainment Weekly*, Wick describes his fascination with "girls marginalized in a man's world who suddenly come into their sexuality and have this enormous power" (Highfill, "Oral History"). Indeed, the creative team behind *The Craft* explicitly and intentionally eschewed any possible Satanic connotations in order to tell a story about growing up and claiming power. Echoing this sentiment, consultant Pat Devin has also expressed a deep understanding of the connection between witchcraft and the adolescent search for self:

> They told me a bit about the movie, that it concerned teenage girls who begin to experiment with magic as a way to attempt to gain power and control their lives. I could understand that, having been a teenager, reading Sybil Leek, singing "Season of the Witch" and joining my high school girlfriends in midnight Ouija Board sessions. (Yohalem)

By explicitly connecting witchcraft to nature and reshaping it as a tool of teenage self-empowerment, *The Craft* portrays witchcraft not as something transgressive, but as a sanctuary for the film's protagonists, a source of strength and solidarity (Greene 165). While this move away from Satanism might suggest a desire to reign in the film's four witches, granting them power only within the gentler, more nurturing realm of Wicca, the creative choice to align witchcraft with non-threatening, nature-based religions massively influenced how mainstream culture understood witchcraft. In an era haunted

59

by the lingering paranoia of the Satanic Panic, *The Craft* reconfigured witchcraft for a popular audience, framing it as something potentially empowering and extricating it from the Satanic anxiety that had engulfed eighties discussions of witchcraft.

BLESSED BE: *THE CRAFT* AND WICCA

Although a complex phenomenon, modern witchcraft can be said to originate with Egyptologist and folklorist Margaret Murray (1863–1963). In her 1921 book The *Witch-Cult in Western Europe*, Murray posited that witchcraft represented the survival of a pre-Christian faith. Although Murray's ideas have since been discredited by most academic historians, her theories were massively influential beyond the academic sphere and directly contributed to the revival of witchcraft in the twentieth century. As Margot Adler observes in *Drawing Down the Moon: Witches Druids, Goddess-Worshippers and Other Pagans in America*, the so-called "witch-cult hypothesis" singlehandedly "generated a number of British covens" (51). Indeed, Murray's claim that this surviving faith was a Dianic fertility cult whose rituals were based in nature and seasonal change was tremendously important to those covens that sprang up in her wake (45). Her work described how witches met at eight major festivals (sabbats) and at more general meetings (esbats) in covens of 13, and this idea has also profoundly impacted the ritual practices of subsequent generations of witches (45).

While Murray's romantic vision of a hidden pre-Christian cult undoubtedly paved the way for the twentieth-century revival of witchcraft, other sources also helped to shape contemporary conceptions of the Craft. James Frazer's *The Golden Bough* (1890), Charles G. LeLand's *Aradia, or the Gospel of the Witches* (1899), Jane Ellen Harrison's *Ancient Art and Ritual* (1913) and Robert Graves's *The White Goddess* (1948) all impacted the development of contemporary pagan witchcraft. These diverse voices contributed to the formation of a distinctly twentieth-century witchcraft tradition. However, aside from Murray, the figure most commonly linked to the rise of the modern Craft is a former civil servant and amateur anthropologist named Gerald Gardner. Born in England in 1884, Gardner was well read in religious studies and occult practices. Following his retirement at the age of 52, Gardner moved first to London and then to the New Forest in the south-east of England (Hutton, *Triumph* 205). It was here that, in 1939, he claimed to have met a local woman called "Old Dorothy" who was the leader of a surviving witch coven of the ancient tradition (205–6). Old Dorothy initiated Gardner into her coven, and by the 1940s he had become increasingly committed to spreading word of the Craft's endurance to the wider world (206).

Following the repeal of Britain's Witchcraft and Vagrancy Act in 1951, Gardner began to give press interviews about his experience with witchcraft. In 1954, he published a book called *Witchcraft Today*, which explicated the practices and beliefs of contemporary witches. In this book, Gardner gives no clue to his own involvement with the Craft, instead posing as an anthropologist interested only in studying witches and correcting public misapprehensions. As Gardner notes in his foreword to the book,

> I have been told by witches in England: "Write and tell people we are not perverts. We are decent people, we only want to be left alone, but there are certain secrets you must not give away." So after some argument as to exactly what I must not reveal, I am permitted to tell as much that has never before been made public concerning their beliefs, their rituals and their reasons for believing what they do, also to emphasize that neither their present beliefs, rituals nor practices are harmful. (*Witchcraft Today* 13)

Although, as Ronald Hutton notes, academic historians are sceptical of Gardner's claims to have discovered a surviving pre-Christian cult, his ideas – like Murray's – have proven enormously influential (Hutton, *Triumph* 206). Gardner played a central role in developing and popularising the religion that would become modern witchcraft. Gardner gave the religion the name "Wica" in *Witchcraft Today*, and by the 1960s it had morphed into the more familiar "Wicca" (Hutton, *Triumph* 241).

Wicca made the transatlantic journey from England to the United States during the 1960s and early 1970s, a time when Gardner's books, alongside those of Murray and Graves, found a large readership amongst the fledgling counterculture (Hutton, *Triumph* 341). The first appearance of Wicca in America can be dated to 1962, when English writer Raymond Buckland and his wife Rosemary arrived in Long Island with a charter from British Gardnerian witches, empowering them to spread word of the Craft in the United States (Russell and Alexander 172). In addition to appealing to the rebellious spirit of the era's counterculture, American witchcraft was also quickly assimilated into the women's spirituality movement and played a prominent role in the radical feminist rhetoric of the 1970s (Hutton, *Triumph* 341). In the same decade, American witchcraft became increasingly organised. The Council of American Witches was founded in 1973. An independent group comprised of members from different witchcraft traditions, the Council published 13 agreed-upon principles of belief that could be said to represent witchcraft as a whole. In 1975, 13 covens came together in northern California to create the Covenant of the Goddess. The Covenant of the Goddess, or COG, emerged out of a desire to build closer bonds between witches, and to unite practitioners of the Craft against possible harassment or persecution (Adler 99). The COG also created a code of ethics whose first principle was derived from the Wiccan Rede, or moral code: "An ye harm none, do as ye will".

In 1979, an American witch, Starhawk (Miriam Simos), published a book called *The Spiral Dance*, which outlined her ideas on what witchcraft is and how it should be practised. *The Spiral Dance* quickly became the best-selling book on the subject of witchcraft, swiftly displacing Gardner's *Witchcraft Today* as the "model text for would-be witches" (Hutton, *Triumph* 345). Starhawk's book was primarily focused on the worship of the Goddess, and in language that would be echoed almost 20 years later in *The Craft*'s description of Manon, *The Spiral Dance* describes how we can connect with the Goddess "through the moon, the stars, the ocean, the earth, through trees, animals, through other human beings, through ourselves. She is here. She is within us all" (346). A few years later, in 1982, the author Marion Zimmer Bradley published the immensely successful *Mists of Avalon*. A reimagining of Arthurian legends, the novel helped to further popularise the notion that witchcraft was an ancient religion, intimately linked to female empowerment (355). Moving beyond the printed text, the rise of internet culture in the 1990s and early 2000s facilitated a marked increase in witchcraft practitioners. Stephanie Martin describes how Wiccan and Pagan groups realised the power of the internet, even as the medium was still in its infancy. Newsgroups like alt. pagan and alt.religion.wicca were established as early as 1995 and private bulletin board services catered to tech-savvy pagans even earlier (Martin 129). Mass market publishers such as Llewellyn Publications also played a major part in bringing Wicca and paganism to a mainstream audience. Llewellyn produced books with a wide market appeal that were readily available in bookstores around the world. Although many witches bemoaned the "Llewellynization" or "dumbing down" of paganism that characterised the eighties and nineties (Lewis, "Pagan Explosion" 19), the simple, non-threatening guides produced by these publishers undoubtedly contributed to Wicca becoming more visible and acceptable. Llewellyn also published a number of witchcraft guides aimed specifically at teenagers and young people, including Silver RavenWolf's *To Ride a Silver Broomstick* (1993) and her later book *Teen Witch: Wicca for a New Generation* (1998).

While *The Craft*'s producer and writers have been explicit about their use of witchcraft as a metaphor for adolescent coming-of-age, the film also reflects a growing, real-world interest in Wicca. Furthermore, *The Craft*'s engagement with existent witchery extends to its use of authentic Wiccan lore and practice. Pat Devin, the film's Wiccan consultant, worked hard to ensure that spells and rites included in *The Craft* aligned structurally, aesthetically and spiritually with those employed by actual witches. In an interview with Douglas Eby, Devin acknowledged the need for creative licence when working on a mass-market horror film:

> It's a motion picture; it's not a documentary, and I did what I could from my end, keeping in mind that the movie deals with four young women who begin to play with magic, and essentially create their own deity. They are not practicing the religion of Wicca. It's sort of "Girls just want to have fun" – girls just want to play with magic.

Despite her awareness of the plasticity of reality in the context of Hollywood cinema, Devin drew heavily on her own experiences as a Wiccan when consulting on the script. In another interview, she stresses that her primary goal for the rituals and chants was that they should be authentic, if generic, and should reflect material found in existing books on witchcraft, or at least appear as though could plausibly have been created by a group of teenage girls (Yohalem). Devin was, for instance, adamant that if the other witches were going to threaten Sarah for deserting the coven, these threats should be legitimised by a preceding scene in which the girls undertook an initiation and committed themselves to one another (Yohalem). Devin took it upon herself to write this initiation scene – the iconic sequence that takes place under the sun-dappled trees of Simi Valley – using "widespread and common wording" (Yohalem). The initiation ritual – wherein the girls take turns to ask one another how they will enter the circle and each responds, "With perfect love and perfect trust" – appears to derive, at least

DEVIL'S ADVOCATES

partially, from the Wiccan Rede. A long version of the Wiccan code of ethics, the Rede, opens with the lines:

Bide the Wiccan Laws ye must In Perfect Love and Perfect Trust.
Live an' let live – Fairly take an' fairly give.

Likewise, the manner in which the girls seal their covenant with one another by depositing a drop of blood in a goblet of wine shared amongst the group is a practice Devin engaged in with one of her own Wiccan congregations.

Devin has confessed that Rochelle, Nancy and Bonnie's search for a fourth member to complete their circle was her idea. She based this narrative conceit on her own women's circle in which a different Priestess calls each one of the four corners – north, south, east and west (Yohalem). The notion that a coven requires four members is, however, entirely fictional. Margot Adler, in an attempt to demystify some of witchcraft's more arcane terms, points out that a coven is simply a "group of people who convene for religious or magical or psychical purposes" (105). While it is not necessary to form a coven in order to practise witchcraft, many witches find spiritual comfort from working with others. Traditional covens usually have 12 or 13 members, although a coven can range in size from three to twenty (105). The girls' search for a "fourth" to complete their circle therefore lacks any basis in reality. Nevertheless, covens generally work in circles or spheres, sacred spaces that contain the magical energies raised during rituals (105). Wiccan rituals usually commence with the creation of this magical circle, and the space is usually purified with the ancient elements: earth, air, fire and water. Again, this aspect of Wiccan spirituality finds its analogue in *The Craft* as Devin assigned each of the four main characters one of these elements. Initially, Devin cast Sarah as Earth, Rochelle as Water (she is a high board diver), Bonnie as fire (because of her burn scars) and Nancy as Air (in Women's circles it is usually the Priestess of the East or Air who controls the rite) (Yohalem). Although *The Craft*'s art department switched Bonnie and Nancy's elements in other scenes, feeling that Nancy better encapsulates the destructive threat of fire (see Introduction), the elemental analogues hold throughout the film and can be seen in characters' wardrobes, personalities and attitudes towards magic.

The representation of the magic circle in the climactic scene during which the girls invoke Manon also has a basis in real magical rituals. The circle is traditionally cast using

64

THE CRAFT

a sword, wand or athame (a small black-handled, double-bladed dagger) (Adler 106). When creating the circle, witches generally employ different symbols to represent the four elements: swords usually represent air, wands embody fire, a cup symbolises water and a pentacle (a disk inscribed with a five-pointed star) signifies earth. In reality, however, it is gods and goddesses, rather than "the Spirit", that are invoked when a circle is cast (106). The words used by Sarah, Rochelle, Bonnie and Nancy during their ritual also have their basis in authentic witchcraft. Many of the phrases they use echo words found in the "Casting the Circle" rite outlined in Doreen Valiente's influential book *Witchcraft for Tomorrow* (1978). In *The Craft*, the girls cast their circle by appealing to the four quarters, with each witch calling to the "guardians" of directional watchtowers, tutelary spirits derived from early modern occult traditions and nineteenth-century esoteric societies:

> NANCY: Hail to the guardians of the watchtowers of the East, the powers of air and invention. Hear me! Us! Hear us!

> BONNIE: Hail to the guardians of the watchtowers of the South, the powers of fire and feeling. Hear us.

> ROCHELLE: Hail to the guardians of the watchtowers of the West, powers of water and intuition. Hear us.

> SARAH: Hail to the guardians of the watchtowers of the North, by the powers of mother and earth. Hear us.

According to Valiente, one should always finish a ritual by closing the circle and thanking the Old Ones for their protection. This should be done by taking a censer of incense, offering it to the four quarters, and stating in turn "Guardians of the East, I thank you. Hail and farewell"; "Guardians of the South, I thank you. Hail and farewell"; "Guardians of the West, I thank you. Hail and farewell"; "Guardians of the North, I thank you. Hail and farewell" (158). In a similar vein, the invocation of the spirit depicted in *The Craft* climaxes with Nancy commanding Manon with the phrase "I summon and stir thee". This too has its basis in existing rites. Valiente's procedure for casting circle features the phrase "I summon, stir and call ye, ye Mighty Ones" (157). In this way, the fictional rituals created for *The Craft*, although having their basis in genuine witchcraft, are far enough

65

removed from the reality of the faith to avoid causing offence or trivialising important religious rites.

The Craft adopts a similar strategy of fictionalisation when it comes to the film's central deity. Wicca is a Neopagan faith, and the beliefs, identifications and affiliations of its adherents can be surprisingly diverse. Different strains of Wicca can comprise members who are theists, agnostics and even atheists. Some Wiccans are monotheists, while others are polytheists. Many Wiccans worship a god and goddess, who serve as complementary opposites, respectively embodying notions of male and female, positive and negative, light and dark. In order to avoid offending real-world witches, the god and goddess do not appear in *The Craft*, nor do any other Pagan deities. Director Andrew Fleming claimed in an interview with the *Guardian* that "We thought it would be more respectful to make a god up". Likewise, Devin is always careful to note that Manon was invented solely for the purposes of the film. When she began working on *The Craft*, each of the four witches had her own name of the Ultimate Deity, and Manon was the name Nancy used (Yohalem). Manon later became the appellation used by all the girls. Devin jokes that when she first read the script, she was amused at the possibility that the "girls were actually invoking the spirit of a pissed off blond French girl who was angry about her father's death" (Yohalem). Devin had, apparently, connected the name to the 1986 film *Manon des Sources* (*Manon of the Spring*). It ultimately transpired that this same film was in fact where one of *The Craft*'s co-writers had found the name.

For as much as *The Craft* transforms existing rituals and conjures up its own imagined deities, the ethical framework evinced in the film is at least partially reflective of Wiccan morality. In *A Witches' Bible*, Janet Farrar and Stewart Farrar stress that Wiccan ethics are positive, guiding rather than prohibitive (135). Witches, according to the Farrars, believe in a "joyful balance of all human functions" (135). This notion of balance also informs the ethical universe of *The Craft*. During the girls' first visit to the magic shop, Lirio tells Sarah that "Life keeps a balance on its own. You understand?" When Rochelle giggles petulantly, Lirio simplifies her lesson: "Well, then, understand this: whatever you send out there you get back times three". The concept of a threefold law is well known in contemporary witchcraft, with many Wiccans holding to the belief that whatever you do returns to you threefold (Adler 109). In *A Witches' Bible*, the Farrars reframe the threefold law as a "Boomerang Effect" (141). As the authors elucidate, "this is the principle, proved time and again, that psychic attack which comes up against a stronger defence rebounds threefold on the attacker" (141). Although not identical, the Boomerang Effect and the threefold law both reflect a basic karmic principle operative in Wicca. Likewise, in *The Craft*, we see the evil deeds of Nancy, Bonnie and Rochelle return to them times three. While Rochelle and Bonnie's punishments are merely illusory, reflected in an enchanted mirror, they are karmically chastised for their wickedness by being stripped of their powers at the end of the film. Nancy, too, is punished for her abuse of witchcraft's power. As Sarah tells her during their climactic confrontation, "[Manon] wanted me to give you a message. You're in big shit. He says you've abused the gifts that he's given you, and now you're going to have to pay the price". Consequently, because Nancy employs magic to manipulate Sarah's perceptions and damage her mental health, she is herself incarcerated in a psychiatric ward at the end of the film. The evil she has magically directed at Sarah has returned to her times three.

In many ways, the idea that one is responsible for the energy they send out into the world fits in well with *The Craft*'s central themes of power and its responsible use. If *The Craft* was born out of Douglas Wick's desire to make a film about four marginalised girls who discover their own inner power, as well as the possible dangers that attend the abuse of that power, then Wiccan ethics are the ideal moral framework through which to explore these themes. Wicca speaks of the responsible use of power, emphasising that individuals are culpable for what they put out into the world. This reflects the process of growing up and learning to act as a responsible agent in the world. As an individual, you can claim power and resist oppression, but it is imperative to use that power responsibly. Witchcraft as both a theme and narrative device in *The Craft* thus provides a useful moral framework through which to teach its young audience about power and responsibility.

NOTES

1. For more on this, see Chapter 1 of my *Witchcraft and Adolescence in American Popular Culture: Teen Witches* (University of Wales Press, 2022).
2. Elements of the Satanic Panic appear to be resurfacing in the early 2020s, with Satanic conspiracies being disseminated via social media and interviews with "SRA survivors" appearing on platforms such as YouTube and TikTok.

Chapter 3: "We are the weirdos, mister": Witchcraft and Identity Politics

In a 2016 interview, recorded to mark *The Craft*'s 20th anniversary, Douglas Wick recalls filming a scene in which the coven, travelling to a remote woodland to conduct their initiation rites, momentarily interacts with three small girls, played by Wick's own daughters (Eggersten). Set to Juliana Hatfield's breathy rendition of "Witches' Song", the sequence sees Bonnie, Rochelle, Nancy and Sarah sitting together at the back of a bus, appearing coolly indifferent to those around them. A cluster of little girls – Wick's daughters – eye the witches with youthful curiosity, and their gaze is returned by Nancy, who lowers her sunglasses and glares menacingly at them. The girls seem unsettled by Nancy's dark clothes and pale visage. Yet, at the same time, there is a suggestion that they are intrigued by the foursome, enchanted by their aloofness and independence. Clad in heavy black or floaty, diaphanous dresses, the witches are presumably unlike any young women the children have ever seen before. With their rebellious demeanour and wilful separation from the other passengers, Nancy, Bonnie, Rochelle and Sarah, embody alternative possibilities for femininity, new ways of experiencing and expressing womanhood.

Figure 11. The witches travel to their initiation. Image: Photofest

Teasing out this notion of difference and diversity, the present chapter contextualises *The Craft* within the broader social transformations of the era in which it was produced. The pages that follow analyse how *The Craft* engages with issues of gender, race, ability and class at a time when these categories of identity were evolving and intersecting in new and dynamic ways. This chapter frames *The Craft* as a product of both postfeminist ideologies and of the third-wave feminism that was beginning to emerge in the 1990s. At the same time, I argue that in as much as *The Craft* is preoccupied with what it means to be a woman in the mid-1990s, it is equally concerned with what it means to a poor woman, a woman of colour or a woman with disabilities. Although numerous think pieces published in the 25 years since *The Craft* was released have both lauded and condemned the film for its treatment of subjects like gender, sexuality, race and class, it is nevertheless a film that earnestly engages with identities and experiences that are too often ignored by mainstream cinema. This chapter, then, concerns itself with how *The Craft* represents, and occasionally fails to represent, adolescent girlhood as an experience shaped not only by gender, but also by race, class and ability.

"POSTFEMINISM" AND "BITCHIFICATION": THE DEMONISATION OF POWERFUL WOMEN

The Craft is a film suffused with complex and often contradictory ideas about womanhood. Produced and set in the mid-1990s, the film's central characters display a certain degree of freedom in their language, dress and behaviour. At the same time, however, the four girls at the heart of the film are constrained by seemingly inflexible notions of femininity, injunctions against promiscuity and impossible aesthetic standards. Both Sarah and Nancy suffer vicious abuse and mockery because of their perceived sexual transgressions – what we would now term "slut-shaming" – while the film's male characters are free to boast of their conquests. This double standard, as well as the way *The Craft* presents its female characters as simultaneously independent and hemmed in by oppressive behavioural constraints, reflects the often-contradictory ideologies of postfeminism.

The Craft was released in 1996, only three years after the neoconservative reign of Ronald Reagan and George H.W. Bush had come to an end. This period of renewed

THE CRAFT

emphasis on "family values" and traditional gender roles witnessed an erosion of women's rights, particularly the reproductive rights carved out by second-wave feminists in the 1960s and 1970s. At the beginning of the 1990s, still in the midst of the Bush presidency, journalist and author Susan Faludi published *Backlash: The Undeclared War Against American Women* (1991). Faludi's book undermines the notion that women's liberation has been a straightforward, unimpeded journey from subservience to equality. Rather, Faludi notes, every advance in women's rights, from the nineteenth-century suffragettes who agitated for voting rights through to the economic independence achieved by working women during the Second World War, has been accompanied by a swift societal pushback. In the 1980s, under the Reagan administration, and the early 1990s, under Bush, this pushback targeted the inroads made by the feminist movement of the 1960s and 1970s.

Faludi argues that not only have politicians attacked reproductive rights and workplace equality, but popular culture too has sought to curtail women's opportunities through stereotyping and mischaracterisation. Early in her book, Faludi observes how in the final decades of the twentieth century women were presumed to have won the battle for equality. Magazines and newspapers in the late 1980s and early 1990s proclaimed that women had "made it": they could "Enrol at any university, join any law firm, apply for credit at any bank" (Faludi 1). At the same time, the media, together with doctors and researchers, also highlighted an epidemic of stress, unhappiness and burnout spreading rapidly amongst the ranks of modern professional women. Popular wisdom connected these phenomena, and the assumption was born that gender equality was the culprit. Women's liberation, it seemed, had rendered women lonely, stressed and unhappy. A narrative emerged suggesting that women were unhappy because they were free: "They had grabbed at the gold ring of independence, only to miss the one ring that really matters" (Faludi 2). During the 1980s, publications ranging from *Vanity Fair* to the *New York Times* blamed female dissatisfaction on the feminist movement (Faludi 3). A *Newsweek* article published at this time condemned feminism as "the Great Experiment That Failed" (Faludi 3).

At the same time, while some commentators have identified the 1990s as thoroughly beholden to conservativism and the anti-feminist backlash of the Reagan and Bush years, others have argued that the era's attitudes towards femininity were infinitely more complex. Angela McRobbie, for instance, claims that both the 1990s and early 2000s were characterised by an "anti-feminist sentiment" which can be distinguished from Faludi's theorisation of a reactionary "backlash against the seeming gains made by feminist activities and campaigns in an earlier period" (McRobbie 1). Instead, McRobbie identifies, in both the politics and popular culture of the period, an incorporation of feminist ideals and rhetoric. However, this incorporation, or "tak[ing] into account", of feminism is bound up with the assumption that the aims of the women's movement have already been achieved, and feminism, as such, is a thing of the past. Consequently, cultural products of this era, from political speeches to popular films, incorporate an ostensibly empowering vocabulary, one that gestures towards concepts of "choice" and "agency", while at the same time converting these ideals into a "much more individualistic discourse" (1). In this way, mainstream culture in the 1990s advocated for (limited) individual empowerment rather than collective political action. McRobbie's argument thus serves to complicate the "backlash thesis" by showing how both politics and culture invoked "freedom" and "choice" as ideals towards which women might aspire, while also framing feminism as "aged" and "redundant" (11).

Employing the example of Helen Fielding's popular "Bridget Jones" newspaper column, which originally ran in the *Independent* and the *Daily Telegraph* between 1995 and 1998, before being adapted into a popular series of novels and films, McRobbie observes how postfeminist discourse frames the ideal modern woman as empowered, but not too empowered. As she goes onto explain, postfeminism in the context of Bridget Jones "seems to mean gently chiding the feminist past, while also retrieving and reinstating some palatable elements, in this case sexual freedom, the right to drink, smoke, have fun in the city, and be economically independent" (12). In a similar vein, Rachel Moseley's article "Glamorous Witchcraft: Gender and Magic in Teen Film and Television" explores how pop cultural representations of the teen witch express a very carefully circumscribed mode of empowerment: "The power of contemporary young film and television witches is glamorous, not excessive and bodily; it is respectable (they are sexy but their bodies are under control and their powers in check), and it is domesticated" (422). Thus, like Bridget Jones and the broader postfeminist rhetoric she embodies, adolescent witches as portrayed in films such as *The Craft*, as well as in television shows like *Sabrina the Teenage Witch* (1996–2003), are powerful. However, their power

THE CRAFT

is controlled, unthreatening and often limited to superficial glamour. Where they do transgress these limitations, these young witches are invariably punished.

As the 1990s progressed, powerful pop culture heroines emerged in television shows such as *Buffy the Vampire Slayer* (1997–2003) and *Charmed* (1998–2006). Embodying the "double entanglement" of postfeminism, these heroines were strong, brave and independent, but rarely threatened ingrained notions of proper femininity. Thus, as Moseley notes, teen witches (and other popular heroines of the period) can be viewed as essentially postfeminist in that they celebrate "the conjunction of female power with conventional modes of femininity, and only in a very circumscribed way, with difference" (419). Women who transgressed these conventions or threatened patriarchal norms in a meaningful way were understood as dangerous, unpalatable "bitches". Indeed, Allison Yarrow argues that the 1990s witnessed an insidious "bitchification" of women who spoke their minds, called out injustice, pursued their sexual desires or traded likeability for success (viii). In her exploration of how the media demonised women like First Lady Hillary Clinton, O.J. Simpson prosecutor Marcia Clark, law professor Anita Hill and White House intern Monica Lewinsky, Yarrow observes how the public narrative surrounding these women excoriated them for their sexuality, or perceived lack of sexuality, indicted them for their ambition, or demeaned them for their inability to adhere to normative femininity (xvi). Yarrow argues that "As women gained power, or simply showed up in public, society pushed back by reducing them to gruesome sexual fantasies and misogynistic stereotypes" (xvi).

A product of this period, *The Craft* has been condemned, retrospectively, for a perceived tendency to punish overly ambitious female characters. From the beginning of the film, Nancy Downs is different from the other girls. While the others cast spells seeking vengeance on bullies, physical beauty or attention from men, Nancy's demands are less tangible. She seeks neither love nor revenge, but rather the power of the film's fictional deity, Manon. Her concerns are not personal but universal and spiritual. Her chanting is always more frantic, her spellcasting more intense than that of her peers. Indeed, it is Nancy who pushes the rest of the coven to invoke Manon. Nancy is more ambitious than her fellow witches, but she is also portrayed as more unstable and bitchier than the others. When Sarah first arrives at St Benedict's Academy, Nancy is overtly cruel to the new girl. Yet, as one *Reel Rundown* article notes, "Sarah is disgusting to Nancy because her

73

life is pretty easy, and yet she mopes and whines. Sarah has a nice home in a nice part of town with a father who loves and respects her". Nancy suffers abuse and poverty, and so her desire for power stems from a need to escape her painful situation. She uses magic to murder two abusive men – would-be rapist Chris and her violent stepfather – and employs witchcraft to improve her family's economic situation. Yet, while the viewer might empathise with Nancy, she is nevertheless cast as the film's primary villain.

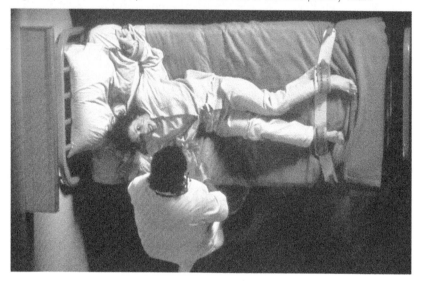

Figure 12. Nancy is punished for her pursuit of power

When Nancy absorbs the power of Manon, it becomes too much for her. She becomes crazed, unable to handle the gifts the deity has bestowed upon her and tries to kill Sarah. Sarah tells Nancy in their final confrontation, "[Manon] says you've abused the gifts that he's given you, and now you're going to have to pay the price". In the end, Nancy does pay the price; she is stripped of her powers and confined to a psychiatric institution (Figure 12). Nancy is a woman whose ambition and thirst for power renders her dangerous and insane, a threat to the stability of the wider social order. The girls in *The Craft* seek power, but Nancy craves too much power and so becomes unstable, dangerous and, ultimately, insane. She is a victim of Yarrow's "bitchification". In the late 1980s and early 1990s, television's perfect woman was, as described in one contemporary report, "beautiful, dependent, helpless, passive [...] and valued for her appearance more than her capabilities and competencies" (Yarrow 2). By 1996, this model had begun to change, as postfeminist rhetoric increasingly touted "choice", "freedom" and "independence", but women on film and television were still expected to be beautiful, good and caring. Nancy's selfish pursuit of power represents a radical break with this ideal, a rupture that was perhaps too radical, as Nancy is villainised and punished for her overweening ambition. Conversely, while Nancy is demonised, or bitchified, for her excessive pursuit of power, for threatening ingrained hierarchies of class and gender, Sarah is celebrated for her carefully delineated use of power. Sarah is smart, strong and independent, but, unlike Nancy, she never challenges societal structures or transgresses dominant notions of proper femininity. Thus, as will be discussed in more detail below, "*The Craft* emphatically privileges a very specific postfeminist conjunction of female power and conventional, hegemonic ideals of white femininity" (Moseley 416).

"GIRLS TO THE FRONT": *THE CRAFT* AND THIRD-WAVE FEMINISM

In the two and a half decades since its release, *The Craft* has received a wealth of retrospective criticism for its treatment of Nancy. In her analysis of the film, Allison Yarrow observes that *The Craft* suggests that "women's extreme power should be constrained or else it will be abused, and that women should be responsible for policing one another" (29). *The Craft* certainly reflects the popular cultural suspicion of overly independent women that thrived in the 1980s and early 1990s, as well as the postfeminist rhetoric that advocated limited power and individual agency. However, despite its often-problematic moralising about the dangers of excessive ambition and corrupting power, *The Craft* is far more nuanced in its treatment of gender, power and female sexuality than many critics realise. *The Craft* is often restrained by the postfeminist "double entanglement" that valorises personal choice and independence at the same time as it relegates the women's movement to the past. However, the film does engage with some of the new forms of feminist activism that were emerging in the 1990s.

When we consider the ebb and flow of feminist activism over the past century or so, we often talk about it in terms of "waves". First-wave feminism can be loosely

75

DEVIL'S ADVOCATES

defined as the nineteenth- and early twentieth-century campaign for women's suffrage. Second-wave feminism emerged in the late 1960s and was primarily concerned with reproductive rights, workplace equality and parity of pay. Today, we talk of the fourth wave, a version of feminism that emerged alongside the growth of online activism and was stoked by the passion of the #MeToo and #TimesUp movements. In the 1990s, when *The Craft* was produced, feminism was experiencing its third wave. The term "third-wave feminism" was coined by activist Rebecca Walker in a 1992 article for *Ms* magazine. Written in the aftermath of law professor and former civil servant Anita Hill's testimony before the Senate Judiciary Committee in 1991, Walker's article was a rallying cry for young women, a passionate reminder that the fight for equality was far from over. In many ways, third-wave feminism can be seen as a response to the dominant postfeminist narrative that framed the women's movement as a thing of the past.

Walker's piece, which seethes with anger and disappointment, was written after conservative nominee Clarence Thomas was appointed to the US Supreme Court despite testimony from Hill claiming he had continually sexually harassed her when she worked for him. The senators who heard her testimony not only appeared incredulous of her claims, but they also mocked her and asked a series of increasingly humiliating questions. Senate Judiciary Committee Chair Joe Biden pressured Hill to discuss the "most embarrassing incidents alleged", while Senator Howell Heflin asked Hill if she was a "scorned woman" (Yarrow 61). Worse yet, Hill was relentlessly mocked by the media, condemned as "a little bit nutty and a little bit slutty" (Yarrow 52). Still in her early 20s, Rebecca Walker wrote in her *Ms* article that "the hearings were not about determining whether or not Clarence Thomas did in fact harass Anita Hill. They were about checking and redefining the extent of women's credibility and power" (Yarrow 39). Moreover, Walker goes on to discuss how the hearings raised important questions such as "Can a woman's experience undermine a man's career? Can a woman's voice, a woman's sense of self-worth and injustice, challenge a structure predicated upon the subjugation of our gender?" (Yarrow 39). Walker argues that the public spectacle of the Anita Hill hearings, Thomas's eventual appointment to the Supreme Court and Hill's demonisation in the media undermined the notion that gender equality had been achieved by previous generations of feminists. Walker states that she, and women like her, must push beyond their rage and articulate an agenda: "I write this as a plea to all women, especially

THE CRAFT

women of my generation: Let Thomas' confirmation serve to remind you, as it did me, that the fight is far from over. Let this dismissal of a woman's experience move you to anger. Turn that rage into political power" (Yarrow 41). Walker concludes her article with the powerful words "I am the Third Wave" (Yarrow 41).

Around the same time, a musical subculture with an intrinsic political bent was emerging in Washington, DC, and the Pacific Northwest, fusing artistic creativity with the social agendas of third-wave feminism. Riot Grrrl was a movement largely comprised of young, white women who defined themselves as feminists and were dissatisfied with the hypermasculine, male-dominated punk scene of earlier decades. Riot Grrrl was made up of bands like Bikini Kill, Calamity Jane, Bratmobile and Heavens to Betsy. The first coherent Riot Grrrl manifesto, authored by the band Bikini Kill in 1990, angrily proclaimed that "Us girls crave records and books and fanzines that speak to US that WE feel included in and can understand in our own ways. […] We are angry at a society that tells us Girl = Dumb, Girl = Bad, Girl = Weak" (Hunt). Riot Grrrl reclaimed femininity as a source of strength. In addition to reclaiming the word "girl", they also reappropriated the derogatory gendered terms like "bitch", "slut", and "cunt" that were often scrawled on their bodies during performances (Lee 64). Likewise, the Riot Grrrl style was defined by reclaimed signifiers of girlhood, often worn with an ironic twist. Riot Grrrls sported hyper-feminine baby-doll dresses worn with clunky combat boots, body piercings, tattoos and smeared lipstick (64). Their dress suggested not only that girlishness could be a badge of honour, but also that there is no single, correct way to be a girl.

In their music, Bikini Kill and other bands railed against patriarchal violence, sexual assault, the erosion of reproductive rights and the oppressive nature of traditional gender roles. Seeking to carve out a place for women in both the music scene and popular culture, Bikini Kill's lead singer Kathleen Hanna would invite all the women at the band's concerts to make their way to the front of the arena, loudly yelling "girls to the front" (Hunt). Likewise, other bands affiliated with Riot Grrrl also fought to expose injustice and improve the lives of women and girls. The band L7, for instance, organised pro-choice benefit concerts around the United States and produced the 1995 "Rock for Choice" CD, which aimed to raise funds for groups committed to reproductive rights (Soccio). Perhaps even more significantly, Riot Grrrl fostered a DIY aesthetic and attitude that encouraged fans to engage in activism themselves. In the early nineties, Riot Grrrl chapters sprang up around the United States. Fans met at conventions where they exchanged homemade publications, bands performed and women held workshops on topics like sexual assault, domestic abuse, eating disorders, self-mutilation, racism and self-defence (Rosenberg and Garofalo 810). The movement thrived both because of these meetings and the popularity of "zines", or homemade magazines. Because zines were written, illustrated, photocopied and distributed by young fans, they did not belong to corporate publishers and as such could explore topics considered too taboo for mainstream women's publications. Zines and Riot Grrrl meetings created a sense of community amongst young women, often college or high school students, who came together to express themselves through art, music and activism. As one young fan claimed in an interview, "Through Riot Grrrl, we can get with people with similar problems and interests, and constructively try to change our world. It's a community, a family" (810).

This sense of sisterly community is central to *The Craft*, and for many viewers it is essential to the film's appeal. Writing on the enduring legacy of *The Craft*, Angelica Jade Bastién observes that more than magic or special effects-laden visions of the supernatural, it is the film's representation of the tender bonds of female friendship that has secured its position as cult classic, particularly amongst women: "The Craft earned a generation of devoted fans because of how it charts the friendship between these four girls – its tentative beginnings, the joys of its strength, and its ultimate downfall – in ways that ring true for any young woman who has had a sisterly connection grow painfully toxic". Rochelle, Bonnie, Nancy and Sarah are outsiders within their small, stifling high school society. Their marginalisation stems largely from economic and cultural factors: race, class, appearance, sexuality. Like the Riot Grrrls of the early 1990s, the four would-be witches are brought together by a shared anger at the injustice inherent in their marginal positions. Dissatisfied with the sexist, racist world they inhabit, the girls carve out their own spaces in which to share their frustrations and support one another. Throughout the film, the four protagonists occupy liminal zones on the edges of their society: they cast spells in empty parks, on beaches, in the forest. Echoing the DIY aesthetic of Riot Grrrl, they build their own community based on the strength of sisterly bonds. In these spaces, they share their experiences of racism, abuse, mental illness and

THE CRAFT

self-harm. They create a safe space where the difficulties of adolescent girlhood can be vocalised – a place of love and support. The girls derive power from this feminine community and reclaim their girlhood as a source of strength. In what is probably the film's most famous scene, Sarah, Nancy, Bonnie and Rochelle step off a bus in an isolated area. As they disembark, the driver turns to the foursome and warns, "Girls, watch out for those weirdos". Nancy lowers her sunglasses and coolly responds, "We are the weirdos, mister". In this moment, Nancy's self-assured response signals that the four witches do not see themselves as vulnerable, potential victims. Instead, they draw strength from their unity; their outsider status has imbued them with a unique power.

That this space of feminine unity serves as a refuge for Sarah, Bonnie, Nancy and Rochelle is hardly surprising, especially considering the diffuse pressures and contradictory messages imbibed by young women in the early nineties. In particular, the 1990s witnessed a marked increase in the objectification of young women in the media, popular culture and the advertising industry. In the late 1990s, Barbara L. Fredrickson and Tomi-Ann Roberts posited the notion of "objectification theory", describing how young women and girls are "acculturated to internalize an observer's perspective as a primary view of their physical selves" (Yarrow 38). Although the objectification of women has long functioned as a corollary of media and the arts, the explosion of new media in the nineties – from the internet to cable television – meant that girls were increasingly confronted with sexualised images of women. Presented largely from a male perspective and for male pleasure, these ubiquitous images of sexualised femininity taught young girls to view themselves from an external, male perspective. As such, they were encouraged to tailor their appearances and present their sexuality for male consumption. Somewhat contradictorily, just as young women found themselves under increased pressure to appear sexually available, they were also being taught that their sexuality was dangerous and shameful. The same year that *The Craft* was released, 1996, abstinence-only education became the default form of sex education in schools across the United States. That year, US President Bill Clinton signed into law legislation that promoted abstinence-only programmes. As part of the Welfare Reform Act, states that provided abstinence-only education would receive lucrative grants of $50 million per annum (Yarrow 31). As a consequence of this, social mores and rituals surrounding sexuality became increasingly convoluted. Because women have historically been viewed

79

DEVIL'S ADVOCATES

as less sexual than men and as having more to lose – socially and economically – from an unplanned pregnancy, they were often cast as the guardians of their own chastity. Boys would always be boys, but girls who engaged in sexual activity were viewed as damaged, dirty or slutty.

This sexual double standard is ubiquitous in The Craft. The film's teenage boys are praised for their promiscuity, while its girls are vilified for engaging in analogous behaviour. In an article on the subject of sexual double standards and adolescent peer acceptance, Derek A. Kreager and Jeremy Staff define the sexual double standard as

> a commonly held belief that sexual behaviors are judged differently depending on the gender of a sexual actor. [...] Boys and men are thought to receive praise and positive attributions from others for nonmarital sexual contacts, while girls and women are believed to be derogated and stigmatized for similar behaviors. (143)

Kreager and Staff describe how, amongst American adolescents, criteria for peer acceptance and popularity (i.e., class background, attractiveness, athleticism, material possessions and prosocial behaviours) were relatively consistent for boys and girls. However, a disparity becomes apparent when we look at sexual behaviours: the social consequences of engaging in sexual activity differ markedly for boys and girls. Girls are punished for sexual activity, while their male peers are lauded for engaging in similar behaviour.

In The Craft this sexual double standard defines the social infrastructure of St. Benedict's Academy and determines its hierarchy. Throughout the film, we see male characters boast about their perceived sexual conquests. Slacker Mitt announces his sexual prowess publicly in French class, informing his teacher and classmates that he got "beaucoup de laid" over the weekend. Chris is equally promiscuous. Nancy warns Sarah early in the film that Chris "spreads disease" and assures her that "I speak from personal experience". The implication is that Chris infected Nancy with an STD. However, Chris is never condemned for his propensity to sleep around. Nancy, on the other hand, is constantly decried as "dirty". Her apparent promiscuity has rendered her a social pariah. Chris even tells Sarah, when he identifies the girls as the "Bitches of Eastwick" that Nancy is a "major slut", suggesting that she is best avoided for this reason. Echoing the punitive language of mid-nineties abstinence-centric sex education, Chris and many of the film's other male characters condemn Nancy for sexual behaviours that they also engage in, suggesting that if she has contracted an STD, then it is she – and not the male partner who infected her – who is at fault. The sexual double standard also emerges in Sarah's relationship with Chris. When Sarah rejects Chris's sexual advances, he nevertheless tells their classmates that the pair slept together and spreads a rumour that Sarah was the "lousiest lay he's *ever* had". Sarah is thus humiliated both for her perceived promiscuity and for the rumours of her inadequacy circulated by Chris. The sense that women are routinely punished for their sexuality is also apparent when Chris, bewitched by a love spell cast by Sarah, attempts to rape her. While she is justifiably traumatised by the experience, she nevertheless blames herself for Chris's actions. Although the film is rather ambivalent in its treatment of this issue, Sarah's unwarranted guilt can be read as a product of a society that positions women as responsible for both provoking and fending off male sexual advances.

The Craft undoubtedly engages with many of the issues that occupied the thoughts and political agendas of third-wave feminists. The film repeatedly alludes to the sexual double standard that sees women condemned for their sexuality while men are praised for it. It also highlights the ubiquity of sexual assault in American culture, alluding to the tragic way women often blame themselves for their own violation. At the same time, however, *The Craft* has received valid criticism for its occasionally ambivalent attitude towards sexual violence. The attack Chris perpetrates against Sarah is framed as the inevitable outcome of the spell she cast. Lirio, the magic shop owner, even stresses the inevitability of whatever consequences arise from the casting of a love spell, telling Sarah that "You unleash something with a spell. There is no undoing; it must run its course". Yet, even this ambiguity, problematic as it may be, situates *The Craft* within the culture of the 1990s and the debates that raged at the time. Although the period may have witnessed resurgent feminist activism and a rising tide of anger about sexual assault, it was also a time of renewed conservatism regarding sex education. Likewise, it was an era when women who spoke out publicly about assault and harassment were widely denounced. *The Craft* reflects all of these discourses simultaneously, embodying some of the period's more unsettling sexism while also making an earnest attempt to expose misogyny and sexual violence and to have conversations about topics that were still widely seen as taboo.

DEVIL'S ADVOCATES

"IF ANYONE IS GOING TO BE A LITTLE BLACK WITCH IN THIS TOWN, IT'S ME": RACE AND RACISM IN *THE CRAFT*

Although *The Craft* is largely preoccupied with the experience of adolescent girlhood and the difficulties inherent in navigating the transition from child to woman, the film also explores how growing up is felt differently by girls from different backgrounds. The four teen witches at the heart of *The Craft* experience female adolescence through the lens of their diverse racial, cultural and socio-economic backgrounds.[1] In particular, for Rochelle, the only witch of colour in the coven, her experience of adolescence and its attendant struggles is inflected by the racism of her classmates and the unique challenges associated with existing in the world as a woman of colour. Rochelle's doubly marginal position is perhaps best expressed in her *seemingly* contradictory role as a Black witch. The term "seemingly" is important here because while witches of colour abound in history and folklore, *The Craft* is, as Heather Greene observes, the first time a Black American witch appears in a prominent role in US cinema. Witches of colour have always formed part of the American popular imagination. During the Salem witch trials of 1692, the bewitchment that swept the small Massachusetts village was initially traced to an Amerindian named Tituba who, despite most likely hailing from South America, has been remembered in literary and popular culture as a Black slave. Representations of Black witches have been further influenced by (largely inaccurate) conceptions of Haitian Vodou and New Orleans Voodoo, as well as folk magic traditions like Hoodoo and rootwork, which have often been conflated with Voodoo in popular culture. Crucially, as Angelica Jade Bastién writes, witches of colour are often portrayed as incidental or supporting characters: "They are used to incite fear or curiosity in the white imagination, which remains deeply suspicious of black ancestral practices that don't allow for easy translation" ("Black Witches").

The fact that cultural representations of Black witches tend to vacillate between comparative invisibility and caricatures informed by racist preconceptions reflects how people of colour have been either erased or presented stereotypically in American horror films. African Americans are largely absent from early Hollywood horror cinema, and where they do appear, they are presented as monstrous, exotic or simply ridiculous. In *Horror Noire*, her groundbreaking study of the Black presence (and absence) in American horror, Robin R. Means Coleman describes the evolution

82

THE CRAFT

of Black representation within the genre. Her study moves from the early days of silent cinema, when white actors in black-face make-up would portray people of colour as either comic foils or animalistic threats to white society, through to the racist conflation of primates and Blacks in films like *King Kong* (1933). Coleman also analyses the comparative invisibility of people of colour during the sci-fi boom of the Atomic Age, an absence which she sees as indicative of the racist belief that the intellectual achievements of this scientific "golden age" were beyond the reach of America's Black population. Furthermore, Coleman pays careful attention to the erasure of Blackness from many of the popular slasher films of the late 1970s and 1980s, arguing that the absence of characters of colour from films like *Halloween* (1978) and *A Nightmare on Elm Street* (1984) speaks volumes about the overwhelming whiteness of America's suburbs and the economic inequality and discriminatory housing policies that created this racial homogeneity.

Rochelle Zimmerman, as played by Rachel True in *The Craft*, is a significant character when read against the history of racist stereotyping and erasure. She is a highly visible presence in the film and is an essential component of the witches' coven. After all, she constitutes one of the four corners necessary for the working of powerful magic. When True originally auditioned for the part of Rochelle, the character was envisioned as a white girl. True auditioned for the role after hearing about it from her friend Jordan Ladd, who had also tried out for the part (Potts). After being told she was "too old" to play the part by her agents, True found a manager who was willing to help her secure the role and over the course of a number of call-backs, the character was reconceived as a woman of colour (Potts). As the character evolved, True became determined that "If anyone is going to be a little black witch in this town, it's me" (Potts). Rochelle is an engaging character largely because she subverts many of the cinematic stereotypes about how a Black woman should be. While Black characters became more prominent in horror films of the 1990s, and a greater number of Black filmmakers began to produce their own movies, there was still a popular tendency to associate these characters with the urban world of the ghetto. Coleman writes that for much of the 1990s,

Blacks were depicted not only as urbanites, but also as living in the inner-city […] Blacks were located in the desolate, ghetto core of the city, quite the opposite of the suburbs or other nonurban places (e.g. the rural). The inner-city became tied to

83

> a racialized and lower socioeconomic image, with Blacks being shown as poor or participating in illegal, underground economies such as drug sales. (175)

Although such images of urban deprivation afforded opportunities for filmmakers to engage in valid and much needed social criticism, the notion of a homogeneous Black culture located solely within the confines of the inner-city is limiting and not reflective of the rich complexity of African American cultures. Rochelle resists a number of pervasive stereotypes about women of colour: she is middle-class, lives in an affluent community and dresses in "goth"-style clothing. Speaking of the joy she felt in playing the part of Rochelle, Rachel True has commented that Rochelle's middle-class upbringing not only reflected True's own experiences, but the character told a different story about the Black experience. In the 1990s, there were, according to True, "like a zillion sort of 'hood' movies", which, while telling a valid story, nevertheless offered a monolithic vision of the Black experience (Eggertsen). True goes on to state that "when I was coming up, I just said, everything I see on TV is like sort of street and urban – 'urban,' and I hate that word – and I just thought, one of the things I wanna do is present characters and portray characters who could be anyone, they just happen to be black" (Eggersten). True's enthusiasm for the character of Rochelle was therefore grounded in the fact that she was not reduced to her Blackness. Her story transcends the typical "urban" setting associated with African American stories at the time. Instead, Rochelle is, for much of the film, simply a teenage girl who happens to be Black.

For many young girls of colour, Rochelle was a liberating character and one viewers could identify with. Ashlee Blackwell, creator of the horror blog *Graveyard Shift Sisters*, writes about the importance of Rochelle to her when she was growing up. Blackwell describes how, as a teenager, "I was constantly confronting micro-aggressions about what kind of Black person I was supposed to be, and wasn't, from all of my peers". She says she was viewed as strange because she didn't conform to popular, stereotypical notions of how a Black girl should look or act. Her primary interests were horror and science fiction, and consequently she failed to embody popular cultural constructions of Blackness. Blackwell recalls that she, and many girls like her, developed feelings of camaraderie towards Rochelle, a character whose Blackness was not defined by the ubiquitous nineties aesthetic of the "ghetto" but rather simply formed part of her complex and multifaceted character. Similarly, Dianca Potts recalls her own adolescent

THE CRAFT

affinity for Rochelle, which developed at a time when "onscreen depictions of black adolescence were few and far between". Potts describes the character of Rochelle as an anchor for her because, like Rochelle, she too grew up in a predominantly white, middle-class environment.

Yet, while Rochelle resists many reductive stereotypes about Blackness, her character is not presented in a colour-blind manner. She references her own racial difference and encounters racism from many of her classmates. In a deleted scene, Nancy explicitly refers to Rochelle as the only Black girl in their school. Moreover, Rochelle's anger and dalliances with malevolent magic directly stem from the racist abuse she suffers from bully Laura Lizzie. Much of Laura's cruelty centres around Rochelle's hair, which she wears in a natural style throughout the film. In one of *The Craft*'s most uncomfortable sequences, Rochelle and Laura are seen getting changed in a school locker room. Laura, about to brush her hair, pauses to examine her brush and exclaims that she has found a "pubic hair" on the brush. She stops again, reconsiders, and announces that it's "just one of Rochelle's little nappy hairs". A heavily racialised word, "nappy" describes "tight kinky Black hair" (Byrd and Tharps 132), and it is often – although not always – used in a derogatory manner to describe an undesirable appearance or texture. That Rochelle is targeted because of her hair makes a great deal of sense, as Black hair has historically been politicised, serving as a microcosm of broader racial attitudes. During the Transatlantic slave trade, captives would often have their heads shaved, an effective method for erasing identities and severing communal bonds in cultures where hair often signified social status, religious affiliation and tribal history. Following the US Civil War and the emancipation of American slaves, hair became increasingly important as a means of integrating with and surviving in a white-dominated society. As Ayana D. Byrd and Lori L. Tharps explain in their history of Black hair, "To gain access to the American dream, one of the first things Blacks had to do was make White people more comfortable with their very presence" (26). Kinky hair was often considered too African. In order to make one's way in a fundamentally racist society, people of colour had to adopt as many Eurocentric traits as possible; they had to fit in with white culture. This was not just a means of succeeding in a white-dominated society, it was often a matter of survival.

Although natural hairstyles became more acceptable, and even fashionable during the Black Power movement of the 1960s and 1970s, individuals who choose to wear their hair in natural styles still face discrimination in schools and workplaces today. A 2019 article published in the *Washington Post* stressed that men and women who wear their hair in natural styles "continue to face implicit or explicit pressures to conform, unwelcome comments or even outright discrimination" (McGregor). Schools and places of employment often penalise people of colour for their natural hair, claiming that it is inappropriate or unprofessional. Consequently, the fact that Laura taunts Rochelle for her "nappy" hair is not incidental; rather, it is reflective of a long and painful history in which hair, alongside other signifiers of racial difference, has been used as a means to single out, oppress and discriminate against people of colour. Although Rochelle ultimately punishes Laura by casting a spell to make her long blonde hair fall out, there is also a tragic sense that Rochelle envies the opportunities afforded to Laura by virtue of her whiteness. Ashlee Blackwell calls attention to a fleeting moment where Rochelle articulates her desire to possess Laura's white privilege. During the scene where the coven is experimenting with glamour magic, just as Sarah has playfully changed her hair and eye colours, Rochelle asks her to "make me blonde". If, as Blackwell argues, Laura's "straight, blonde locks were a symbol in itself of an idealized status of social capital, supposed racial superiority and prosperity", Rochelle's plea to "make me blonde" suggests that she desires to occupy, even momentarily, Laura's privileged position.

Rochelle is certainly one of *The Craft*'s more complex characters. She defies prevalent stereotypes about Black Americans and is in many ways simply a teenager who happens to be Black. She is happy and proud of who she is, but at the same time she desires the social privileges afforded to her white peers. It is this level of nuance that has endeared Rochelle to so many viewers and made her an emotional anchor for many young Black girls who grew up watching *The Craft*. At the same time, while Rochelle is never reduced to a stereotype, many viewers, as well as actress Rachel True, have complained that her motivations are largely dominated by her experience of racism. Ashlee Blackwell, for instance, laments the fact that Rochelle seems to be afforded less screen time than her white peers and that a scene featuring Rochelle's parents was cut – after all, we meet Sarah's, Nancy's and Bonnie's parents. In an interview with *Hitfix*, Rachel True notes that in the film, each of the witches has a specific issue motivating her use of dark magic. For Rochelle, True explains, her issue is grounded almost entirely in her race. Although True is careful to clarify that Rochelle's race is an issue only for

THE CRAFT

others and that Rochelle is not ashamed of who she is, many commentators have felt that reducing her motivations to the experience of racism does diminish the character, particularly in light of the fact that Rochelle is the only one of the four who does not seem to have a family or a home life. It is also unfortunate that Rochelle's struggle against racist bullying seems to have eclipsed other facets of the character that were present in the original script. The character of Rochelle was originally conceived of as battling with anorexia and bulimia, and while True recalls thinking, "Yeah, that's so not me" (Potts), it seems unfortunate that the removal of this plot point appears to have coincided with the character's reconfiguration as a Black girl. The excision of Rochelle's eating disorder is regrettable because the implication appears to be that problematic relationships with food are solely a white, middle-class issue. Indeed, this is a stereotype that has persisted for as long as eating disorders have been in the public eye: the typical anorexic or bulimic is portrayed as a thin white girl from an affluent background. In reality, though, eating disorders affect people of all genders, ages and socio-economic backgrounds. Significantly, eating disorders are equally prevalent amongst people of colour as they are amongst whites, although rates of misdiagnosis and underdetection are higher amongst people of colour (Herrin). Moreover, while Rochelle is never defined solely by her race, the fact that her motivations are reduced to the experience of racist bulling undermines some of Rochelle's complexity, particularly when compared to the rich backstories afforded to the other girls. Nevertheless, *The Craft*'s exploration of the insidious nature of racism and its ubiquity amongst the affluent middle classes exposes the many prejudices still active in the supposedly progressive 1990s. The fact that Rachel True herself was initially excluded from the film's publicity junket, a decision which she describes as seeming "a little racist back then, to be honest" (Potts), and later left out of conventions and reunions, also suggests that the film's representation of systemic, ingrained racism continues to be of relevance.

"SHE DOESN'T WANT TO BE WHITE TRASH ANYMORE": NANCY AND ECONOMIC INEQUALITY

In as much as Rochelle's experience of adolescent girlhood is shaped by her racial identity, her sister witch Nancy Downs is equally defined by her socio-economic

DEVIL'S ADVOCATES

background. As noted above, Nancy is immediately presented as different from her peers. She stands out not just from her classmates, but from her fellow witches as well. Nancy is more intense and her commitment to witchcraft more ardent. When she chants and casts spells, she does so with an urgency that borders on fanaticism. Nancy also appears to be the leader of the coven, often cutting down other members in an attempt to assert her dominance over the group. Her ruthlessness is evident at numerous points throughout the film but is perhaps most apparent in the scene where the four girls attempt to invoke the spirit of Manon. Not only does Nancy, as the group's leader, speak first, but she also reveals her own selfish intentions. While the spell calls for unity, with each witch calling out to the guardians of the watchtowers to "hear us", Nancy initially implores them to "hear me". Although she swiftly corrects herself, Nancy's use of the word "me" betrays her desire for individual power – she wants Manon to favour her. Nancy, more than any of the other witches, is consumed by a quest for power and loses herself in the ecstasy of that power when it is granted to her.

When considering why Nancy might be so single-minded in her pursuit of power, it is important to consider her socio-economic background and how she has been shaped by experiences of depravation and abuse. The first time we see Nancy's home, she is returning amid a rainstorm to the trailer she shares with her mother and stepfather. The interior of the trailer is small and cluttered. As the deluge continues, the electrical supply cuts out and the trailer is plunged into darkness. Nancy's mother, Grace, loudly reprimands her husband for failing to pay the electricity bill, and when he responds that the power cut is a result of the storm, the two begin to fight loudly. The image of Nancy's home life as deprived and dysfunctional accords with popular conceptions of the working class, particularly as they were portrayed in the media of the period. After the recessions of the 1980s and very early 1990s, the American economy began to improve and by the mid-1990s many Americans wished to see themselves as upwardly mobile. In order to maintain this vision, popular culture and political rhetoric of the period increasingly cast the poor, those trapped in cycles of economic disadvantage, as the Other. Indeed, as David Simmons observes in his study of class in American horror fiction, the period from the 1980s onwards has seen a move away from an understanding of the poor as fellow humans, people "like us" who simply lost their way, towards a belief that the "poor are fundamentally different"; "that they

THE CRAFT

live in a different way with different values and models of behaviour; and that this is their choice" (2). Many Americans have come to believe that there exists a "culture of poverty" (2), a lifestyle to which the poor willingly adhere or fail to escape from due to laziness, ignorance or corruption. Consequently, while the 1970s and 1980s witnessed the growth of economic inequality and the disappearance of opportunities for social mobility that culminated in "Reagan's 'trickle down' economics" (121), popular culture often portrayed (and continues to portray) the poor as deprived due to personal failings rather than as a result of discriminatory social and economic policies or practices.

Nancy's family certainly conforms to this vision of the poor as a "*cultural* Other" (Gandal 3). Both Nancy's mother and her stepfather appear to be alcoholics, they fight constantly and are depicted as sloppy and untidy, a visual cue that suggests laziness. Moreover, this conception of poverty as a culture or state of mind, rather than the result of misfortune or systemic inequality, can also be seen after Nancy and her mother join the ranks of the middle classes. Following Nancy's use of magic to dispatch her abusive stepfather, she and her mother receive a $175,000 life insurance pay-out. Rather than using the money to live a moderate, "respectable" life, Nancy and Grace buy a fashionable, expensive luxury apartment (but still wear trashy clothes) and frivolous items like a jukebox that plays "nothing but Connie Francis records". The implication here seems to be that while Nancy and her mother now possess adequate finances, they still live in a "culture of poverty" because they lack the sense and moral refinement to manage their new finances responsibly.

Nancy's thirst for power is reflective of the environment in which she has grown up. Her desire to escape her working-class origins thus fuels Nancy's ardency and her obsessive pursuit of Manon's gifts. When Nancy first tells Sarah about Manon's power, she explains that "It's like you take him into you. It's like he fills you. He takes everything that's gone wrong in your life and makes it all better again". Sexual subtext aside, Nancy's words make it clear that her desire for Manon is grounded in her belief that he will save her from the deprivation and abuse that has been her lot in life so far. When Sarah retorts, "Nothing makes everything all better again", Nancy says, "Maybe not for you". Nancy's meaning here is clear: while Sarah has suffered the legitimate pains of mental illness and suicidal ideation, her life is comparatively comfortable and safe. Sarah struggles with mental illness, and this should not be minimised, but she also has a father and stepmother who love her dearly. She lives a safe and stable life in a home provided by her parents. Conversely, Nancy lives in a trailer that appears on the verge of collapse. Her parents seem lost in an alcoholic daze and her stepfather sexually assaults her. For Nancy, witchcraft is an escape, and the power of Manon offers a way out of the life in which she will otherwise remain trapped.

Nancy uses her magic to secure two things: socio-economic advancement and the power of Manon. However, for her, these two desires are interrelated. During the initiation ceremony, when the witches drink wine and speak their desires under the protective boughs of an ancient tree, Nancy asks for "all the power of Manon". Later, when Bonnie and Sarah ask about Nancy's initiation spell, Rochelle tells them, "She doesn't want to be white trash anymore". Rochelle's use of the term "white trash" is significant because it situates Nancy within a broader history of American poverty. "White trash" is a surprisingly old insult. According to Anthony Harkins, the term first appeared in print in the United States during the 1830s, although its vernacular use probably pre-dates this (367). The phrase was originally used by people of colour to refer to white Americans who did not own slaves, but it was later adopted by the white upper classes to denigrate poor whites (367). While the term "white trash" is predicated on the racist assumption that non-white people are trash by default (Donnella), the existence of a specific term to demean poor white Americans also belies the myth of American equality. Indeed, without magic it seems that someone like Nancy might never escape poverty because America lends the poor few opportunities to better their socio-economic position

Nancy's personality, her ambition and her cruelty are informed by her earlier experiences of poverty, and it is perhaps for this reason that many viewers of *The Craft* do not see Nancy as the villain she was clearly intended to be. In a piece for *Vice* magazine, Alana Massey frames Nancy as "a hero" for dispatching would-be rapist Chris and empathises with her difficult personal circumstances. As a character, Nancy is shaped by her class background. Her experience of female adolescence, while in some ways analogous to that of her peers, is also different, deformed by her exposure to poverty, abuse and the hopelessness of deprivation. Nancy, is like so many women who thirst for power, ultimately destroyed by that power. The film's ending suggests that she must be punished not only for her destabilisation of gendered norms – she is a threat to the postfeminist ideal of appropriate, limited feminine power – but also because she desires to transcend the social position into which she has been born.

"I TAKE INTO MYSELF THE POWER TO BE BEAUTIFUL, OUTSIDE AS WELL AS IN": TRAUMA IN BODY AND MIND

Scars, both emotional and physical occupy a central position throughout *The Craft*. Each of the girls possesses a unique psychic trauma that informs her practice of magic and her attitude towards the Craft itself. However, two of them also sport visible, physical scars. Sarah initially bonds with Bonnie, Nancy and Rochelle after they notice the scars visible on her wrists following a failed suicide attempt. Sarah's scars serve as a physical manifestation of her mental turmoil and the residual guilt she experiences about her mother's death in childbirth. Sarah also experiences flashbacks to her suicide attempt, suggesting a lingering trauma surrounding the event. In an interview with the *Huffington Post*, director and co-writer Andrew Fleming recalls an incident in college where a girl in his dormitory attempted suicide and he found her with her wrists slashed (Jacobs and Brucculieri). By refashioning this difficult memory into the personal history of the film's protagonist, Fleming also touched upon a new concern that had emerged in the 1990s: the propensity of troubled young people to self-harm (See Chapter 2). Self-injury and suicidal ideation drew an unprecedented degree of attention from parents, psychologists and educators in the early 1990s. Where psychiatric professionals had previously viewed self-injury as indicative of other disorders, a symptom of a related disease, during the 1990s, they began to study self-harm as a unique phenomenon (Yarrow 209). Amongst young women, cutting was the dominant mode of self-injury, and this is reflected not only in Sarah's suicide attempt, but in Bonnie's familiarity with the practice of wrist cutting, which suggests that she has also attempted suicide or engaged in self-harm. Allison Yarrow observes that psychologists in the 1990s came to believe that self-harm served as a coping mechanism for many young girls, who used physical pain to express difficult emotions (210). While Sarah's suicide attempt appears bound up with her guilt about her mother's death in childbirth, Bonnie's interest in, or recourse to, self-harm may indicate a desire to take control over her own pain. In Bonnie's case, however, her suffering is not solely psychological, she also occupies a body that is scarred, suffering and visibly different from the bodies of her peers.

When we first encounter Bonnie she is swathed in layers of heavy clothing. Her sweaters have high necks, and her loose coat appears to envelop her small, fragile figure. She moves as though she wishes to render herself invisible. Bonnie keeps her head down, her face often obscured by her stringy hair, and holds her schoolbooks tightly and protectively against her chest. The reason for Bonnie's introverted stance and behaviour is revealed early in the film. Speaking in the hushed tones of high school rumour, Chris informs Sarah that Bonnie has scars covering her body, noting that while he hasn't seen them, friends of his have. In a 2016 interview, Andrew Fleming recalls that this aspect of Bonnie's character was based on a girl he knew in college who had scars covering large sections of her body. Her scars, like Bonnie's, were never visible, as she was able to hide them beneath her clothing. However, for Fleming, the fact that these much-discussed scars were hidden "made it weirder" (Eggertsen). Reflecting this experience, Bonnie, who apparently suffered severe burns in her youth, is widely gossiped about; her scars taking on mythic proportions because they are rarely, if ever, seen by others.

Bonnie's scars have and continue to cause her an immense degree of physical pain. When Bonnie commences treatment intended to lessen her scarring, described in the film as an experimental form of gene therapy, we catch a glimpse of this suffering as the procedure is painful and invasive, involving repeated incisions with a needle that cause Bonnie to scream in agony. However, while Bonnie suffers physically, she also struggles with the psychological effects of her disfiguring scars. Her introverted personality is presented as a direct result of her scarring. She is marginalised by the fascination and revulsion her classmates exhibit towards her scarred body, and her self-esteem is damaged by a failure to embody rigid standards of female beauty. In this way, Bonnie's experience of teenage girlhood is shaped by her disfigurement or disability in much the same way that Rochelle's and Nancy's experiences of adolescent femininity are informed by race and class. Although disability is generally defined as a limitation that interferes with the performance of everyday tasks like walking, moving, seeing, hearing, breathing and learning, modes of being that do not significantly impair the individual, such as certain mental illnesses and disfigurement, can lead to discrimination and limit an individual's capacity to perform routine activities (Schmiesing 191). Consequently, while Bonnie is not impaired, she experiences discrimination, cruelty and marginalisation as a result of her disfigurement. Rosemarie Garland-Thomson, one of the founding scholars of disability studies, argues that beyond notions of impairment, "such culturally generated and perpetuated standards as 'beauty,' 'independence,' 'fitness,' 'competence,' and 'normalcy' exclude and disable many human bodies while validating and affirming others" (7). Bonnie, through her inability to conform to socially constructed notions of "beauty" and "normalcy" is thus excluded and disabled. Her disfigurement prevents her from establishing healthy social relationships, from dating and from dressing in fashionable, revealing clothes like other girls her age. Bonnie is therefore cut off from society, and aside from her fellow witches, is unable to develop meaningful social connections with her peers.

Bonnie's emotional and psychological trauma is extensive, and so, when she asks Manon to give her "the power to be beautiful, outside as well as in", she is pleading for respite from her internal suffering as well as from her external disfigurement. Bonnie draws on the power of the coven to heal her disfigurement and following a number of spells and rituals her scars fall away during a course of her gene therapy. Returning to school after the dissolution of her scars, Bonnie wears revealing sweaters and short skirts, showing off the body she had once so carefully concealed. Her confidence also increases. She becomes flirtatious, at one point lasciviously cat-calling an attractive man in the street: "Don't be shy honey. Nice ass!" Sarah jokes that she is a "slut", but later severely reprimands Bonnie, telling her that, before her scars healed, "You used to be nice". Sarah's discomfort with Bonnie's newly outgoing, extraverted persona echoes the postfeminist ambivalence *The Craft* also displays with regard to Nancy's ambitious desire for power and Sarah's experience of sexual assault. Although widely condemning the manner in which women are marginalised, oppressed and rendered vulnerable, even in modern America, the film also reflects some of the more conservative attitudes prevalent during the time of its production, evincing a distrust of overly ambitious women and suggesting that girls can invite sexual assault through their behaviours or intentions. Bonnie's confidence, while initially presented as positive, is ultimately framed as crossing a line into meanness or aggression. Responding to accusations that she has become narcissistic, Bonnie states that she has lived most of her life as a "monster", and now that she is freed from the conspicuous Otherness of her disfigurement, she is going to relish that freedom.

Bonnie's words here are telling; she considers her previous appearance monstrous, and this certainly aligns with dominant cultural constructions of disfigurement. Ann Schmiesing observes that even in fairy tales, the earliest narratives many of us are exposed to as children, "physical ability or beauty" is employed as a symbolic marker "to accentuate a character's moral virtues or other positive traits", while physical impairment, deformity or disfigurement is used as "a mark that signifies evildoers or further ostracizes the marginalized" (1). Cinema has also, historically, utilised disfigurement as a visual shorthand for evil. During the silent era, when information was primarily conveyed visually, films like *Nosferatu* (1922), *The Phantom of the Opera* (1925) and *The Man Who Laughs* (1928) framed disfigurement or "ugliness" as a physical manifestation of "moral depravity or evilness" (Kirby). In later cinematic productions, where the advent of sound removed the necessity of conveying information solely in visual terms, representations of disfigurement became more complex. Male heroes, for instance, could now possess minor disfigurements or scars and still retain their heroic status (Kirby), while female characters who suffered disfigurements were ruined, destroyed or as good as dead. The central character in Georges Franju's 1960 film *Eyes Without a Face* occupies a state of living death because her facial scarring has erased her identity and cut her off from society. Bonnie's assertion that she has lived most of her life as a monster is therefore reflective of a cultural standard according to which disfigurement is generally aligned with moral depravity, and disfigurement in a woman results in social ostracisation. While male attractiveness is certainly prized, men are valued for a host of diverse traits: strength, leadership, intellect, wit, etc. If their physical attractiveness is spoiled in some manner, they may still possess other attributes valued by their culture. Women, however, have consistently been reduced to their physical bodies. Women who fail to adhere to rigid aesthetic standards are denigrated and ostracised. Unlike a man who suffers disfigurement, a woman whose appearance has been marred is viewed as having lost everything. Bonnie seems all too aware of this when she expresses joy at being released from her previous status as a "monster", a social non-entity who has failed to embody the beauty demanded of her as a woman. Bonnie's excessive confidence, although characterised by Sarah as narcissistic, reflects her sense of liberation. Yet, the fact that Bonnie is vilified for her new-found confidence again suggests that women can go too far.

GOING TOO FAR: COMPLEX AND CONTRADICTORY
REPRESENTATIONS OF EMPOWERMENT

The Craft employs witchcraft as an analogue for female empowerment, yet the film frames this empowerment as a delicate balancing act. Strength and confidence are portrayed as admirable traits in a young woman, and the ability to break free from abusive patriarchs and pervasive objectification is presented as empowering. Yet, *The Craft* nevertheless suggests that a woman can go too far, become too powerful, too confident or too vengeful. Again, this harkens back to the postfeminist "double entanglement" discussed by McRobbie, where individual agency is lauded, but any actual threat to patriarchal (and, by extension, white supremacist) political structures is swiftly denounced. It is perhaps for this reason that Sarah occupies the role of the film's nominal hero. The other girls are framed as excessive in their desires. Nancy's thirst for power is overwhelming, Rochelle's revenge against her bully becomes too cruel and Bonnie's confidence transforms into arrogance. *The Craft* therefore presents Sarah, the only natural witch in the group, as the only one capable of moderating her desires and wielding her powers responsibly. Indeed, by the end of the film, Sarah is the only one allowed to keep her newly discovered abilities. Although aspects of this conclusion suggest that *The Craft* is in many ways a morality tale about the responsible use of power (See Chapter 1), a number of critics have argued that it seems somewhat unfair that Sarah – the white, middle-class, able-bodied witch – is the only one to retain her powers, the only one presented as possessing the wisdom to use them responsibly. Certainly, this is problematic and reveals implicit cultural bias in terms of how the media construct ideals of "goodness" and "heroism".

Nevertheless, *The Craft* is an engaging and important film because of the way in which it presents each of its central characters as shaped by their diverse identities. Rochelle is not just a teenage girl, she is a Black teenage girl; Nancy is not just a teenage girl, she is a working-class teenage girl; Bonnie is not just a teenage girl, she is a teenage girl with a serious disfigurement. Each of these young women experiences the world through the lens of diverse identificatory categories. Consequently, *The Craft* is a unique example of 1990s teen cinema in that it presents its main characters in a manner that could be considered "intersectional". The term "intersectionality" was coined in 1989 by legal scholar Kimberlé Crenshaw as a means of articulating how "race, class, gender, and other individual characteristics 'intersect' with one another and overlap" (Coaston). As people, how we experience and navigate the world around us is not determined by our affiliation with a single identity, e.g., our race, sexuality, gender, class, etc. Instead, our experiences and opportunities are determined by the intersection of these different identities. Consequently, the way a Black man experiences the world will be different from the way a Black woman experiences the world; the way a working-class lesbian experiences the world will differ from the way a middle-class queer person will experience the world. People cannot be reduced to a single identity, rather we are all influenced by a host of different factors, from race and ethnicity to class, gender and sexuality. *The Craft* is an innovative film because it presents the teenage girls at the centre of its narrative as informed not simply by their status as adolescent girls, but also by their race, class and ability.

As noted above, however, the film has been criticised for vilifying its Black, working-class and disabled witches, only allowing a white, middle-class, able-bodied girl to be a natural witch with the capacity to wield power in a responsible, judicious manner. This is certainly a valid criticism, and while it could be countered that Sarah herself is shaped by her struggles with mental illness, the film does appear to privilege whiteness, middle-class values and bodily integrity. In her discussion of the film, Alexandra West laments that

> While the film discusses racism and the insidiousness of the bullying associated with it, it feels too easily dismissed. At the end of the film, Sarah can walk away from the power and horrors that she has just experienced, but other characters cannot. Her ability to walk away highlights her privilege while also undermining the very real issues that a character like Rochelle faces. (41)

The Craft is therefore a complex film, one that attempts to fight against the prejudices of its era while at the same time reinforcing them. Although the four witches at the centre of the film struggle against inequality and social injustice, certain aspects of the text reinforce racial and class-based hierarchies. In places, *The Craft* also appears to reflect rather than challenge cultural narratives that blame women for the sexual assaults and harassment they experience. Likewise, while the film champions female empowerment, it also expresses an anxiety about how this empowerment might go too far. However, the very fact that it portrays female empowerment, while also presenting a diverse image of adolescent girlhood, suggests that *The Craft*'s intentions were inclusive, progressive and genuinely concerned with countering the reductive, one-dimensional images of young women that abounded in popular culture of the period.

NOTES

1. I also explore issues of race, class and ability in *The Craft*, albeit from a different perspective, in Chapter 4 of my *Witchcraft and Adolescence in American Popular Culture: Teen Witches* (University of Wales Press, 2022).

CONCLUSION

INVOKING THE SPIRIT: THE LEGACY OF *THE CRAFT*

The Craft was released into the world in 1996, a year rich in fictional representations of adolescent witches. Writing for the *AV Club*, Sinead Stubbins christened 1996 "the year of the teen witch". While *The Craft* appeared in late spring, by autumn, *Sabrina, the Teenage Witch* had made its debut on ABC, and a cinematic adaptation of Arthur Miller's seminal play *The Crucible* was released theatrically in the winter. While *Sabrina* and the 1996 version of *The Crucible* have both been influential in their own right, *The Craft*'s nuanced portrayal of contemporary teenagers gaining power from occult forces has had the most potent influence over subsequent portrayals of teen witchery. Although *The Craft* was not a phenomenal box office success, it garnered a massive cult following once it was released on VHS. The film struck a chord with teenage girls, and many found themselves trying to levitate friends at candlelit sleepovers and imitating the goth style of Nancy, Bonnie, Rochelle and Sarah.

Plans to expand the world of *The Craft* were discussed, but ultimately fell through. The actors who played lead roles in the film had sequels written into their contracts, and director/screenwriter Andrew Fleming wrote a sequel and a television pilot based on *The Craft*. Sadly, neither of these projects was ever developed and *The Craft*'s legacy would come to reside primarily in the immense influence it exerted over subsequent media. The most direct and explicit pop cultural reworking of *The Craft* was Aaron Spelling's drama series *Charmed*, which ran on the WB network from 1998 to 2006. Like *The Craft*, *Charmed* centres around a group of young witches, who, despite their seemingly ordinary appearance, possess immense power. *Charmed* deviates from *The Craft* in that its protagonists are not teenagers, but young women in their 20s. The three witches, Prue (Shannen Doherty), Piper (Holly Marie Combs) and Phoebe (Alyssa Milano), are also literal, as opposed to figurative, sisters, and all share the same white, middle-class upbringing. Another derivative of *The Craft* is the US–Canadian film *Little Witches*. Released in late 1996, *Little Witches* has a plot that is very similar to *The Craft*, and it is also set in a Catholic school.

DEVIL'S ADVOCATES

More creative responses to and reiterations of *The Craft* can be found in popular late-1990s teen television series like *Buffy the Vampire Slayer*. While *Buffy* was already in production in 1996, when *The Craft* was released, and was based on a 1992 film of the same name, it nevertheless bears traces of *The Craft*'s pop cultural influence. Witches appear in the show's first series, filmed in 1996, but they are villainous and loosely defined creatures. These witches owe much to stereotypical constructions of witchcraft as sinister and evil; they practise their craft using a confusing melange of voodoo dolls and boiling cauldrons. In season 2, which ran from 1997 to 1998, witchcraft is represented in a more nuanced manner, with its connections to Paganism rendered far more explicit. This season sees one of the show's main characters, Willow Rosenberg (Alyson Hannigan), develop an interest in witchcraft. Over the next five seasons, as Willow's involvement with the occult becomes increasingly central to her character, witchcraft is linked more explicitly with the kind of Wiccan practices depicted in *The Craft*.

Later television series featuring teen witches also employed thematic and aesthetic features drawn from *The Craft*. The third season (2013–2014) of anthology series *American Horror Story* is set in a New Orleans academy for adolescent witches. Not only does the titular coven's aesthetic frequently recall that of *The Craft* – its main characters hew closely to a goth style, frequently wearing diaphanous black clothing, chunky boots and dark sunglasses – but the series also mirrors some of *The Craft*'s key thematic concerns. The coven at the centre of the show reflects the intersectional dynamic of *The Craft*, featuring witches of differing ethnicities, socio-economic backgrounds and abilities. *AHS: Coven* also employs witchcraft as a metaphor through which to explore the experience of adolescent girlhood, and it engages with often difficult themes, including racism, sexual violence and bullying. The popular Netflix series *The Chilling Adventures of Sabrina* (2018–2020) also owes a clear debt to *The Craft*. Despite being directly influenced by the Archie Comics property *Sabrina the Teenage Witch* and Roberto Aguirre-Sacasa's dark comic book series *The Chilling Adventures of Sabrina* (2014), certain elements of the series bear traces of *The Craft*'s pervasive cultural influence. In particular, the Weird Sisters, a trio of vaguely gothic teen witches, echo *The Craft*'s supernatural clique. Like *The Craft*, *Chilling Adventures* also utilises witchcraft as an imaginative framework through which to explore serious social and cultural issues, in this case, relating to queer identities, class and fourth-wave feminism.

100

THE CRAFT

Although *The Craft* did not by any means invent the archetype of the teen witch – adolescent girls have been entangled with the occult since the Salem witch trials – its fusion of witchcraft lore and adolescent strife has made it a potent imaginative brew. For young women, in particular, witchcraft is an appealing metaphor for the adolescent experience. As Sinead Stubbins has argued

> The teen witch doesn't reject the teen girl experience; if anything, the trope embraces the strange magic and intensity of female friendship. It challenges a society that both limits the power of young women and perceives them to be naturally limited. By having supernatural strength, these characters can defy a social structure that equates female adolescence with weakness and vulnerability.

With its love spells and capacity for magically assisted metamorphosis, witchcraft is a strange, distorted mirror of adolescence, of its intense crushes and its uncontrollable biology. At the same time, witchcraft appeals to teenage girls, perhaps more than it does to any other segment of the population, because the Craft offers power. Teen girls are often doubly disenfranchised. As both child and woman, the adolescent girl inhabits two identities historically cut off from social or political power. Teenage girls are often characterised in popular culture as silly, frivolous or superficial. Their interests and passions, from *Twilight* to One Direction, are regularly maligned as shallow. Characterising a film, television show or musical act as "for teen girls" has become critical shorthand for a lack of seriousness or depth. Witchcraft, therefore, frequently appears in fiction as the only route towards power and self-determination for young women who are regularly dismissed and demeaned by the culture they inhabit.

Perhaps it is this promise of power that has led *The Craft* to endure in the popular imagination. Over 20 years after the film's initial release, Anne Cohen wrote that *The Craft* has only become more relevant. In the aftermath of the 2018 Brett Kavanaugh hearings, when yet another powerful man was admitted to the US Supreme Court despite being accused of sexual assault, Cohen argued that the figure of the witch offers hope to women when it seems that the vast, immovable infrastructures of culture and politics are all massed against them: "Too often, women feel powerless to change circumstances – political, social, financial, take your pick – that feel beyond their control. *The Craft* presents a universe in which any slight could magically be made right, and in

101

our current climate, that's an appealing prospect".That witchcraft offers women the ability to challenge, to fight back against, the structures that have oppressed and that harm them, may explain why both witchcraft in general and *The Craft* in particular hold a special place in the hearts of many women. The witch is, after all, a symbol of resistance. She is a woman who, lacking any meaningful political, social or economic influence of her own, turns to the only forces that welcome and protect her: nature, the earth, her sisters.

The Craft has enjoyed a vibrant afterlife in popular culture, music and fashion. In her article, Cohen observed that in 2018 a cursory Instagram search for "#TheCraft" returned over 192,000 results that ranged from GIFs of the film's most iconic scenes to tattoos, fan art, *Craft*-inspired fashion shoots and more. In the same year, popular US clothing brand Urban Outfitters was selling an oversized, retro t-shirt emblazoned with the faces of the film's four main characters. In 2019, alternative clothing brand Hot Topic debuted a line of fashion based on *The Craft*. Featuring everything from replicas of the film's "suspender" skirts and rosary-bead necklaces to themed hoodies and "Invocation of the Spirit Book Wallets", the popular range had everything an aspiring witch might need to recreate the film's most iconic ensembles. In 2013, singer Kary Perry released a song entitled "Dark Horse", which she claimed was directly inspired by *The Craft*. Featuring lyrics including, "So you wanna play with magic/Boy, you should know whatcha falling for" and "Mark my words/This love will make you levitate", Perry has explained in interviews that the song is "about warning a guy that if you're going to fall in love with me, make sure you're sure because if not, it's gonna be your last" (Rutherford). Two years later, in 2015, the girl group Little Mix released the witchcraft-themed song "Black Magic". Not only did the song's lyrics centre on occult enchantments, but the video, clearly based on *The Craft*, featured four teen girls discovering magic and using their new powers to win over their crushes and punish school bullies.

The enduring popularity of *The Craft* can also be seen at fan conventions and cast reunions. Three of the film's stars – Neve Campbell, Robin Tunney and Rachel True – appeared at a special Halloween screening of the film in LA's famous Hollywood Forever cemetery in October 2013. A few months earlier, San Francisco's landmark theatre, The Castro, played host to "*The Craft* Witch-tacular". Hosted by drag performer and filmmaker Peaches Christ and *Rupaul's Drag Race* winner Sharon Needles, the "Witch-

THE CRAFT

tacular" comprised a screening of *The Craft* and a pre-show musical extravaganza. Promotional material for the event bore the tagline "Now is the time. This is the hour. Drag is our magic. Drag is our power!" The show was a tribute to the original 1990s film, with gothic drag queens lip-syncing and dancing to songs from *The Craft*'s soundtrack. Both irreverent and loving, Peaches Christ's tribute act is also a reminder that *The Craft* has long nurtured a devoted fanbase in the LGBTQ+ community.

The Craft's cultural cache is also visible in the fact that while rumours of a remake or sequel abounded for over two decades, filming on a remake was finally completed in early 2020. Produced by Blumhouse, *The Craft: Legacy* was released on streaming platforms in October 2020 but received little fanfare from either fans of the original or critics in general. *Legacy* was intended as a sequel/quasi-reboot of the 1996 film. Helmed by director Zoe Lister-Jones, the film centres on a new group of adolescent witches and, like the original, employs witchcraft as a metaphor for the teenage experience. *The Craft: Legacy* also deals with difficult facets of high school life, including bullying, sexism and homophobia. The young cast is strong, but the sequel ultimately lacks the tension of the original, as none of this new generation of young witches finds herself drawn to the dark side. Indeed, Lister-Jones's film explicitly addresses some of the criticisms levelled at the original film, particularly complaints about the way it portrayed female friendships as volatile and prone to cattiness. In *The Craft: Legacy*, the young witches do not turn on each other, but instead confront an external, male villain in the form of an evil warlock (played by David Duchovny). Certainly, this attempt to avoid regressive portrayals of female bitchiness is laudable, but both the villain and the film's mythology seem underdeveloped. Ultimately, *Legacy* feels like a brief introduction to the world of witchcraft, and it often seems more like a television pilot than a complete movie. This is unfortunate because its characters are fascinating, and the viewer is left wanting more. Lister-Jones also endeavours to rectify some of the original's more stereotypical or reductive representations of gender, race and sexuality, but these themes also remain underdeveloped. We learn, for instance that one of the witches, Lourdes (Zoey Luna), is trans, but this is only mentioned briefly, and we never really get to know her character. Witchcraft expert and media scholar Peg Aloi alludes to the fundamental superficiality of the film when she notes in her review that "*The Craft* portrays witchcraft as alluring, complex and consequential: in *The Craft: Legacy*, witchcraft is fashionable, quick to master, and easily renounced" ("Featherlight Reboot"). *Legacy*, although an admirable attempt at a twenty-first-century reimagining of *The Craft*, ultimately lacks the complexity of the original.

Despite the lukewarm reception of the sequel, *The Craft* remains an iconic and influential film. Perhaps one of the most enduring facets of *The Craft*'s immense influence is its power to draw young people to real-world witchcraft. More than its legions of devoted fans, more than the profound influence it exerted over subsequent cultural representations of witchcraft, *The Craft* is a film that confronted a generation of young people with new spiritual possibilities. Peg Aloi has argued in her study of the media's influence on contemporary witchcraft that *The Craft* has been the biggest influence on the growth of teenage witchcraft in modern America ("Charming Spell" 118). Aloi observes that after *The Craft* was released in theatres, some pagan writers cautiously praised its use of both authentic ritual texts and its implicit warning about dabbling in magic for personal gain, while simultaneously condemning its use of special effects to portray magic as a superficial illusion (118). Nevertheless, Aloi, along with many other pagans, was surprised by how many young people were drawn to paganism as a direct consequence of seeing the film (118). Jeffrey B. Russell and Brooks Alexander likewise call attention to the surge of adolescent interest in the occult that followed *The Craft*'s theatrical release. "The effect", they note, "was explosive and virtually instantaneous" (182). Just a few days after the film opened, witchcraft and Neopagan groups began to receive queries from curious teens. This surge of interest initially proved problematic, as few practising witches at the time had experience of working with young people. Most Wiccan and Neopagan groups lacked any kind of infrastructure appropriate to the needs of teenagers and almost none of them had organised teen outreach programmes (182). In the aftermath of the 1980s Satanic Panic, many witchcraft groups were skittish about the possibility of engaging with young people, fearful of the legal ramifications that might attend parental accusations of corruption. As such, many teenagers were left to cobble together an understanding of witchcraft from popular culture, friends and internet sources. That being said, publishers, including Llewellyn (discussed in Chapter 2), swiftly stepped in to fill the gap, and by 1998 Silver RavenWolf's *Teen Witch: Wicca for a New Generation* had hit the shelves. While many of the teenagers who embraced witchcraft in the late 1990s, inspired by *The Craft* or *Buffy the Vampire*

THE CRAFT

Slayer, may have later discarded the faith, others remained devoted. Even those who abandoned witchcraft along with other relics of their rebellious youth came away from the experience more educated about the occult and more empathetic towards other beliefs. *The Craft* is therefore an important film, not merely from a cinematic perspective, but spiritually and socially. It directly contributed to a massive demographic shift in the late 1990s wherein huge numbers of teenagers exchanged traditional religious practices for witchcraft. It opened up new horizons, new ways of seeing the world for generations of young people, and its legacy endures even into the twenty-first century.

BIBLIOGRAPHY

Adler, Margot. *Drawing Down the Moon: Witches, Druids, Goddess-Worshippers, and Other Pagans in America*. Revised and updated edition, Penguin, 2006.

Aloi, Peg. "A Charming Spell: The Intentional and Unintentional Influence of Popular Media upon Teenage Witchcraft in America." *The New Generation Witches: Teenage Witchcraft in Contemporary Culture*, edited by Hannah E. Johnston and Peg Aloi, Ashgate, 2007, pp. 113–27.

———. "*The Craft: Legacy* is a Featherlight Reboot Where *The Craft* Was a Cult-Hit Addiction." Polygon, 28 October 2020. www.polygon.com/2020/10/28/21539033/the-craft-legacy-review-sequel-reboot. Accessed 10 September 2021.

Aloi, Peg, and Hannah E. Johnston. "Introduction." *New Generation Witches: Teenage Witchcraft in Contemporary Culture*, edited by Hannah E. Johnston and Peg Aloi, Ashgate, 2007, pp. 1–9.

Alvarez Sesma, Griselda. "A Short History of Tonantzin, Our Lady of Guadalupe." *News From Indian Country*, 2008. https://web.archive.org/web/20190306043309/https://www.indiancountrynews.com/index.php/news/education-life/6538-a-short-history-of-tonantzin-our-lady-of-guadalupe. Accessed 10 December 2022.

Ash. "1996s 'The Craft': Why Nancy Was the True Hero." *ReelRundown*, 13 October 2018. https://web.archive.org/web/20210616012841/https://reelrundown.com/movies/Why-Nancy-was-the-True-Hero-of-1995s-The-Craft. Accessed 10 December 2022.

Bastién, Angelica Jade. "The Profound, Enduring Legacy of *The Craft*." *Vulture*, 27 October 2017. www.vulture.com/2017/10/the-craft-its-enduring-legacy.html. Accessed 10 April 2020.

———. "Why Can't Black Witches Get Some Respect in Popular Culture?" *Vulture*, 31 October 2017. www.vulture.com/2017/10/black-witches-why-cant-they-get-respect-in-pop-culture.html. Accessed 15 April 2020.

Behringer, Wolfgang. *Witches and Witch-Hunts: A Global History*. Polity Press, 2004.

DEVIL'S ADVOCATES

Blackwell, Ashlee. "20 Years of The Craft: Why We Needed More of Rochelle." *Graveyard Shift Sisters*, 16 November 2016. www.graveyardshiftsisters.com/blog//2016/11/20-years-of-craft-why-we-needed-more-of.html. Accessed 10 December 2022.

Bradley, Marion Zimmer. *The Mists of Avalon*. Alfred A. Knopf, 1982.

Brannon, Linda. *Gender: Psychological Perspectives*. 7th ed., Routledge, 2017.

Brennan, Judy. "'The Craft' Has the Knack for Scaring up an Audience." *Los Angeles Times*, 6 May 1996. www.latimes.com/archives/la-xpm-1996-05-06-ca-1108-story.html. Accessed 23 April 2020.

Byrd, Ayana D., and Lori L. Tharps. *Hair Story: Untangling the Roots of Black Hair in America*. St. Martin's Publishing, 2001.

CanLit Guides. "Postfeminism." https://web.archive.org/web/20210303173814/https://canlitguides.ca/canlit-guides-editorial-team/postfeminism-and-conservative-feminism/postfeminism/. Accessed 8 April 2020.

Chandler, Emily, "'Loving and Cruel, All at the Same Time': Girlhood Identity in *The Craft*." *Girlhood Studies*, vol. 9, no. 2, 2016, pp. 109–25.

Clover, Carol J. *Men, Women, and Chain Saws: Gender in Modern Horror Film*. Princeton University Press, 1992.

Coaston, Jane. "The Intersectionality Wars." *Vox*, 28 May 2019. www.vox.com/the-highlight/2019/5/20/18542843/intersectionality-conservatism-law-race-gender-discrimination. Accessed 19 April 2020.

Cohen, Anne. "In Troubled Times, We Turn to Witches – & *The Craft* Led the Way." *Refinery29*, 25 October 2018. www.refinery29.com/en-us/2018/10/214496/the-craft-review-underrated-teen-witch-movie. Accessed 23 April 2020.

Coleman, Robin R. Means. *Horror Noire: Blacks in American Horror Films from the 1890s to Present*. Routledge, 2011.

Cowan, Jared. "Revisiting the L.A. Filming Locations of *The Craft* Twenty Years Later." *LAWeekly*, 2 May 2016. www.laweekly.com/revisiting-the-l-a-filming-locations-of-the-craft-20-years-later/. Accessed 16 August 2019.

THE CRAFT

Davies, S.F. "The Reception of Reginald Scot's Discovery of Witchcraft: Witchcraft, Magic, and Radical Religion." *Journal of the History of Ideas*, vol. 74, no. 3, 2013, pp. 381–401.

de Blécourt, Willem. "Witches on Screen." *The Oxford Illustrated History of Witchcraft and Magic*, edited by Owen Davies, Oxford University Press, 2017, pp. 253–80.

Dickson, Andrew. "How We Made *The Craft*." Interview with Andrew Fleming. *Guardian*, 1 March 2016. www.theguardian.com/film/2016/mar/01/how-we-made-the-craft-horror-movie-interview. Accessed 16 August 2019.

Donnella, Leah. "Why Is It Still OK To 'Trash' Poor White People?" *WLRN*, 1 August 2018. https://www.wlrn.org/2018-08-01/why-is-it-still-ok-to-trash-poor-white-people. Accessed 10 December 2022.

Doyle, Sady. "Season of the Witch: Why Teenage Girls Are So Dang Scary". *Rookie*, 14 October 2011. www.rookiemag.com/2011/10/the-season-of-the-witch/. Accessed 16 August 2019.

Driscoll, Catherine. *Teen Film: A Critical Introduction*. Bloomsbury, 2011.

Ebert, Roger. "Reviews: The Craft." 3 May 1996. www.rogerebert.com/reviews/the-craft-1996. Accessed 31 July 2019.

Eby, Douglas. "Interview with Pat Devin about Consulting on the Movie: 'The Craft.'" https://web.archive.org/web/20071113145924/https://talentdevelop.com/interviews/pdevin.html. Accessed 15 December 2019.

Eggertsen, Chris. "'The Craft' Turns 20: Rachel True, Andrew Fleming and Douglas Wick on the Making of a Teen Classic." *Uproxx*, 3 May 2016. https://uproxx.com/hitfix/the-craft-turns-20-rachel-true-andrew-fleming-and-douglas-wick-discuss-the-making-of-a-teen-classic/. Accessed 12 March 2020.

Ewens, Hannah. "How 'The Craft' Realized the Power of Teen Girls and Made Witchcraft Cool." *Vice*, 3 May 2016. www.vice.com/en_us/article/vdqmp3/revisiting-the-craft-the-film-that-realised-the-monstrous-power-of-teen-girls. Accessed 10 April 2020.

Faludi, Susan. *Backlash: The Undeclared War Against American Women*. Crown, 1992.

Farrar, Janet, and Stewart Farrar. *A Witches' Bible*. FW Media, 1996.

Fitzpatrick, Anna. "Everything I Need to Know About Growing up I Learned from Supernatural Teen Movies." *Rookie*, 17 October 2011. www.rookiemag.com/2011/10/high-school-supernatural/. Accessed 16 August 2019.

Fleming, Andrew, director. *The Craft*. Sony 1996.

Gandal, Keith. *Class Representation in Modern Literature and Film*. Palgrave Macmillan, 2007.

Gardner, Gerald. *Witchcraft Today*. Citadel Trade, 1954.

Garland-Thomson, Rosemarie. *Extraordinary Bodies: Figuring Physical Disability in American Culture and Literature*. Columbia University Press, 1997.

Gaskill, Malcolm. *Witchcraft: A Very Short Introduction*. Oxford University Press, 2010.

Gateward, Frances, and Murray Pomerance. "Introduction." *Sugar, Spice, and Everything Nice: Cinemas of Girlhood*, edited by Frances K. Gateward and Murray Pomerance, Wayne State University Press, 2002, pp. 13–21.

Gibson, Marion. *Witchcraft Myths in American Culture*. Routledge, 2007.

———. *Witchcraft: The Basics*. Routledge, 2018.

Greene, Heather. *Bell, Book and Camera: A Critical History of Witches in American Film and Television*. McFarland, 2018.

Grossman, Pam. *Waking the Witch: Reflections on Women, Magic, and Power*. Gallery Books, 2019.

———. "The Wizard of Oz Invented the 'Good Witch.'" *Atlantic*, 25 August 2019. www.theatlantic.com/entertainment/archive/2019/08/80-years-ago-wizard-oz-invented-good-witch-glinda/596749/. Accessed 30 December 2019.

Hall, Elaine J., and Marnie Salupo Rodriguez. "The Myth of Postfeminism." *Gender and Society*, vol. 17, no. 6, 2003, pp. 878–902.

Harkins, Anthony. "Hillbillies, Rednecks, Crackers, and White Trash." *The New Encyclopedia of Southern Culture*, edited by Anthony Harkins, vol. 20, *Social Class*. University of North Carolina Press, 2012, pp. 367–70.

THE CRAFT

Heller-Nicholas, Alexandra. "'The Only Word in the World Is Mine': Remembering Michelle Remembers." *Satanic Panic: Pop-Cultural Paranoia in the 1980s*, edited by Kier-La Janisse and Paul Corupe, FAB Press, 2015, pp. 19–31.

Herrin, Marcia. "What Does the Research Say about Ethnicity and Eating Disorders?" *Psychology Today*, 30 July 2011. www.psychologytoday.com/ie/blog/eating-disorders-news/201107/what-does-the-research-say-about-ethnicity-and-eating-disorders. Accessed 16 April 2020.

Highfill, Samantha. "The Craft: Fairuza Balk Shuts Down Those Witch Rumors." *Entertainment Weekly*, 16 October 2017. https://ew.com/movies/2017/10/16/the-craft-fairuza-balk-witch-rumors/. Accessed 23 March 2020.

———. "We Are the Weirdos, Mister: An Oral History of *The Craft*." *yahoo!entertainment*, 17 October 2017. www.yahoo.com/entertainment/weirdos-mister-oral-history-craft-193043498.html. Accessed 23 September 2019.

Hunt, El. "A Brief History of Riot Grrrl – the Space-Reclaiming 90s Punk Movement." *NME*, 27 August 2019. www.nme.com/blogs/nme-blogs/brief-history-riot-grrrl-space-reclaiming-90s-punk-movement-2542166. Accessed 7 April 2020.

Hutton, Ronald. *The Triumph of the Moon: A History of Modern Pagan Witchcraft*. Oxford University Press, 1999.

———. *The Witch: A History of Fear, from Ancient Times to the Present*. Yale University Press, 2017.

Jacobs, Matthew, and Julia Brucculieri. "Relax, It's Only Magic: An Oral History of 'The Craft.'" *Huffington Post*, 20 May 2016. www.huffpost.com/entry/the-craft-oral-history_n_5734f7c9e4b060aa7819d362. Accessed 16 August 2019.

Janisse, Kier-La. "Introduction: Could It Be Satan?" *Satanic Panic: Pop-Cultural Paranoia in the 1980s*, edited by Kier-La Janisse and Paul Corupe, FAB Press, 2015, pp. 13–17.

Kearney, Mary Celeste. "Girlfriends and Girl Power: Female Adolescence in Contemporary U.S. Cinema." *Sugar, Spice, and Everything Nice: Cinemas of Girlhood*, edited by Frances Gateward and Murray Pomerace, Wayne State University Press, 2002, pp. 125–42.

Kempley, Rita. "*The Craft*: Far from Crafty." *Washington Post*, 3 May 1996. www.washingtonpost.com/wp-srv/style/longterm/movies/videos/craft.htm. Accessed 23 April 2020.

Kirby, Philip. "Battle Scars: *Wonder Woman*, Aesthetic Geopolitics and Disfigurement in Hollywood Film." *Geopolitics*, vol. 25, no. 4, 2018, pp. 916–36.

Kreager, Derek A., and Jeremy Staff. "The Sexual Double Standard and Adolescent Peer Acceptance." *Social Psychology Quarterly,* vol. 72, no. 2, 2009, pp. 143–64.

LaSalle, Mick. "High School Is Really Hell: Co-Eds Cast Spell in 'The Craft,'" 3 May 1996. *San Francisco Chronicle*. Accessed 22 April 2020.

Lee, Christina. *Screening Generation X: The Politics and Popular Memory of Youth in Contemporary Cinema*. Ashgate, 2010.

Levack, Brian P. *The Witch-Hunt in Early Modern Europe*. 4th ed., Routledge, 2016. EPUB.

Levy, Emanuel. Review: "The Craft." *Variety*, 1 May 1996. https://variety.com/1996/film/reviews/the-craft-2-1200445935/. Accessed 10 December 2022.

Lewis, James R. "The Pagan Explosion: An Overview of Select Census and Survey Data." *New Generation: Teenage Witchcraft in Contemporary Culture*, edited by Hannah E. Johnston and Peg Aloi, Ashgate, 2007, pp. 13–23.

———. "Satanic Ritual Abuse." *The Oxford Handbook of New Religious Movements*, 2nd ed., edited by James R. Lewis and Inga B. Tollefsen, e-book edition, Oxford University Press, 2016, 2 vols. EPUB.

Lottermoser, Katie. "Subcultures and Scenes: Riot Grrrl." Grinnell College, n.d. https://haenfler.sites.grinnell.edu/subcultures-and-scenes/riot-grrrl-2/. Accessed 7 April 2020.

McGregor, Jena. "More States Are Trying to Protect Black Employees Who Want to Wear Natural Hairstyles at Work." *Washington Post*, 19 September 2019. www.washingtonpost.com/business/2019/09/19/more-states-are-trying-protect-black-employees-who-want-wear-natural-hairstyles-work/. Accessed 16 April 2020.

McRobbie, Angela, *The Aftermath of Feminism: Gender, Culture and Social Change*. Sage, 2009.

Mankey, Jason. "Pagan Time Capsule: 1990's." *Patheos*, 12 August 2014. www.patheos. com/blogs/panmankey/2014/08/pagan-time-capsule-90s/. Accessed 18 December 2019.

Martin, Stephanie. "Teen Witchcraft and Silver Ravenwolf: The Internet and Its Impact on Community Opinion." *The New Generation Witches: Teenage Witchcraft in Contemporary Culture*, edited by Hannah E. Johnston and Peg Aloi, Ashgate, 2007.

Massey, Alana. "Boring Sarah Is the True Villain of 'The Craft.'" *Vice*, 31 October 2017. www.vice.com/en_us/article/vb3bam/boring-sarah-is-the-true-villain-of-the-craft. Accessed 17 April 2020.

Moseley, Rachel. "Glamorous Witchcraft: Gender and Magic in Teen Film and Television." *Screen*, vol. 43, no. 4, 2002, pp. 403–22.

Muir, John Kenneth. *Horror Films of the 1990s*. McFarland, 2011.

Orenstein, Peggy. "The Movies Discover the Teen-Age Girl." *New York Times*, 11 August 1996. www.nytimes.com/1996/08/11/movies/the-movies-discover-the-teen-age-girl.html. Accessed 5 August 2019.

Palmer, William J. *The Films of the Nineties: The Decade of Spin*. Palgrave Macmillan, 2009.

Pearson, Jo. "Witchcraft Will Not Soon Vanish from This Earth: Wicca in the 21st Century." *Predicting Religion: Christian, Secular and Alternative Futures*, edited by Paul Heelas Grace Davie and Linda Woodhead, Routledge, 2003, pp. 170–83.

Pipher, Mary. *Reviving Ophelia: Saving the Selves of Adolescent Girls*. Riverhead Books, 1994.

Potts, Dianca. "The Lenny Interview: Rachel True." *Lenny*, 30 March 2018. www. lennyletter.com/story/the-lenny-interview-rachel-true. Accessed 16 April 2020.

Purkiss, Diane. *The Witch in History: Early Modern and Twentieth-Century Representations*. Routledge, 1996.

RavenWolf, Silver. *Teen Witch: Wicca for a New Generation*. Llewellyn Publications, 1998.

———. *To Ride a Silver Broomstick: New Generation Witchcraft*. Llewellyn Publications, 1994.

Rosenberg, Jessica, and Gitana Garofalo. "Riot Grrrl: Revolutions from Within." *Signs*, vol. 23, no. 3, 1998, pp. 809–41.

Russell, Jeffrey B., and Brooks Alexander. *A New History of Witchcraft: Sorcerers, Heretics & Pagans: Sorcerers, Heretics and Pagans.* 2nd ed., Thames & Hudson, 2007.

Russell, Sharon. "The Witch in Film: Myth and Reality." *Planks of Reason: Essays on the Horror Film*, edited by Barry Keith Grant and Christopher Sharrett, Scarecrow Press, 2004.

Rutherford, Kevin. "Katy Perry Reveals 'Prism' Influences, Adds Stripped-Down Performances at Album Release Event." *Billboard*, 22 October 2013. www.billboard.com/articles/columns/pop-shop/5763220/katy-perry-reveals-prism-influences-adds-stripped-down. Accessed 23 April 2020.

Schmiesing, Ann. *Disability, Deformity, and Disease in the Grimms' Fairy Tales.* Wayne State University Press, 2014.

Shary, Timothy. *Generation Multiplex: The Image of Youth in Contemporary American Cinema.* University of Texas Press, 2002.

Simmons, David. *American Horror Fiction and Class: From Poe to Twilight.* Palgrave Macmillan, 2017.

Smith, Andy W. "'These Children That You Spit On': Horror and Generic Hybridity." *Monstrous Adaptations: Generic and Thematic Mutations in Horror Film*, edited by Richard J. Hand and Jay McRoy, Manchester University Press, 2007.

Soccio, Lisa. "From Girl to Woman to Grrrl: (Sub)Cultural Intervention and Political Activism in the Time of Post-Feminism." *[In]Visible Culture: An Electronic Journal for Visual Studies*, no. 2, 1999. https://www.rochester.edu/in_visible_culture/issue2/soccio.htm. Accessed 10 December 2022.

Sternadori, Miglena. "The Witch and the Warrior: Archetypal and Framing Analyses of the News Coverage of Two Mass Shootings." *Feminist Media Studies*, vol. 14, no. 2, 2014, pp. 301–17, www.tandfonline.com/doi/abs/10.1080/14680777.2012.739571. Accessed 10 December 2022.

Stubbins, Sinead. "'We Are the Weirdos, Mister': *The Craft* and the Year of the Teen Witch." *AV Club*, 3 May 2016. https://film.avclub.com/we-are-the-weirdos-mister-the-craft-and-the-year-of-1798246863. Accessed 31 July 2019.

Thurston, Robert W. *The Witch Hunts: A History of the Witch Persecutions in Europe and North America*. Routledge, 2007.

Troy, Gil. *The Age of Clinton: America in the 1990s*. Thomas Dunne Books, 2015.

Valiente, Doreen. *Witchcraft for Tomorrow*. Robert Hale, 1978.

Walker, Rebecca. "Becoming the Third Wave." *Ms* 39 (1992), pp. 39–41.

West, Alexandra. *The 1990s Teen Horror Cycle: Final Girls and a New Hollywood Formula*. e-book edition, McFarland, 2019. Kindle.

Wood, Robin. "Teens, Parties, and Rollercoasters: A Genre of the 90s." *Hollywood from Vietnam to Reagan … And Beyond*. Revised edition, Columbia University Press, 2003, pp. 309–32.

Yarrow, Allison. *90s Bitch: Media, Culture, and the Failed Promise of Gender Equality*. Harper Perennial, 2018.

Yohalem, John Brightshadow. "An Interview with Pat Devin, Consultant For 'The Craft,'" *The Library*, March 1998. https://web.archive.org/web/20190312185150/http://wychwoodacastlebetweentheworlds.com/interviewWithPatDevin.htm. Accessed 10 December 2022.